E

s Critics

World
d

ce
tieth

uals,

Inquiry

by the

arty

Comparative Study

merican

Program

litical

Constitutional Language

AN INTERPRETATION OF JUDICIAL DECISION

John Brigham

Contributions in Political Science, Number 17

GREENWOOD PRESS
WESTPORT, CONNECTICUT　●　LONDON, ENGLAND

Library of Congress Cataloging in Publication Data

Brigham, John, 1945-
  Constitutional language.

  (Contributions in political science ; no. 17
ISSN 0147-1066)
  Bibliography: p.
  Includes index.
    1. United States—Constitutional law—
Interpretation and construction. 2. Judicial
process—United States. 3. Law—Language.
I. Title. II. Series.
KF4550.B73   342'.73'02014   78-4020
ISBN 0-313-20420-9

Library of Congress Catalog Card Number: 78-4020
ISBN: 0-313-20420-9
ISSN: 0147-1066

First published in 1978

Greenwood Press, Inc.
51 Riverside Avenue, Westport, Connecticut 06880

Printed in the United States of America

10 9 8 7 6 5 4 3 2 1

Contents

Constitutional Language

which in turn throws "light on the question how far reality is intelligible."[9] The method depends in part on answering "the question of how language is connected with reality."[10] The answer is pure Wittgenstein. "There is no way of getting òutside the concepts in terms of which we think of the world."[11]

In Charles Taylor's article, "Interpretation and the Sciences of Man,"[12] these traditions are joined in a critique of the social sciences that posits the existence of "intersubjective meanings" as a key to social action left unexplained by empirical social science. We cannot explain the meaning of social institutions like voting without attention to the basic dimensions of social life represented by them. John Gunnell's recent work focuses on the inadequacies of what he calls the "logical positivist/empiricist analysis of the logic and epistemology of science,"[13] which he finds represented in the approaches of Dahl, Easton, and Deutsch.[14] It is in large part adherence to a positivist conception of linguistic meaning that perpetuates a stance on "the relationship between normative and empirical assertions,"[15] which has limited the predominant mode of political analysis. Gunnell presents a new interpretation of the activity of political philosophy which is equally relevant to research on political institutions and public policy. This kind of research has been undertaken in some vivid investigations of the role of language in political life.

A number of works, such as Lakoff's *Language and Women's Place*[16] and Edelman's *Political Language,*[17] demonstrate how language maintains the society in its present state by encouraging people to see that state as the natural order of things. Edelman relies on Chomsky to establish the framework that "perception involves categorization."[18] He sees categorization as an activity influencing the political arena in such specific contexts as the interaction between bureaucrats and recipients in the welfare system, as well as citizen perception of the system. Others, like Claus Mueller in *The Politics of Communication*[19] and William E. Connolly in *The Terms of Political Discourse*[20] demonstrate the general characteristics of language as it applies to politics. Mueller's work portrays language as "the main agent of man's integration into a culture."[21] The symbol system of language creates "a social bond between individuals and groups,"[22] and differentiates groups and classes in society. In his presentation, the linguistic codes reflect group socioeconomic conditions. He portrays language as the key to thought processes and conceptual possibilities. The political implications that he pursues are the arrested and constrained capacities of certain groups and the collective belief systems that are the basis of social demands and the authority of the state. Connolly's book advances similar claims and describes study of the prevailing terms of political discourse as "a dimension of politics itself."[23] His objective is to begin the enterprise of political research through study of these terms. His approach recognizes that the social theorist makes his most important contribution by interpreting how language operates rather than by urging precision. The message is essentially that the way we see the world determines what is politically possible and that the world—with its richness and its oppression—is contained in our language. Indeed, the promise of attention to language by students of symbols is that the investigation of such large and amorphous political considerations as ideology might be broken down into components, thereby revealing the structure through which politics operates.

Although language is the most dramatic expression of the human capacity to live by and manipulate symbols, in the political realm symbols are most carefully recorded in the law. In the legal sphere, precise accounting of how symbols are used is an important convention facilitating investigation. It is thus reasonable to turn to law as a place where language manifests itself. It is not surprising that many students of politics or politically relevant issues have already converged there.

The interest which H.L.A. Hart showed in the special status of legal epistemology opened the way for investigations that move from the fact-value dichotomy.[24] He noted that legal terms like "corporation" are neither reality nor fiction. Such concepts have a dual role. They guide judicial decision not simply as norms but because of the meaning they convey. Hart's major work[25] was influenced by the analysis of language undertaken by his philosophical contemporaries in England. His successor, Ronald Dworkin, moves even further from the conception of the law as governed by rules. Dworkin's insight into the conventions which give meaning to law is also closely related to the symbolic processes existing in language.[26]

Gidon Gottlieb, in *The Logic of Choice*, covers much of the jurisprudential literature that delineates what students of law have had to say about judicial decision.[27] This literature should be studied by anyone wishing to understand characterizations of this form of political action based on philosophical work with language.[28] Judicial decision looks to reasoning with rules. The present study, however, sees the judicial decision in the Supreme Court as characterized by reasoning where, although the outcome stands as rules, the basis for choice itself is comparable to the use of language. While Gottlieb stretches the theory and method of logical analysis to incorporate modern theories concerning the operation of symbolic processes, I have sought to avoid the constraints of rules in the decision by looking at a level of judicial decision that is not always governed by clear rules. Where rules are operative, we must indeed pay greater attention to the unique problems they raise. However, the present study examines a context where rules seldom exist as clear guides to action. This is indeed the basis for a distinction between the model herein proposed and that employed by role theorists. Like behavioral studies which make no reference to legal rules, the study of linguistic dimensions of the decision builds on action rather than on norms. (The distinction from the behavioral tradition is that the observations are of the symbolic dimensions of action.) Gottlieb, however, masterfully attacks the positivist dichotomy (addressed most directly in Chapters 2 and 3 of this volume). He notes the difficulty of fitting legal philosophy into this scheme.[29] He is also careful to avoid the "messianism inherent in the move to a new method," preferring to suggest insight not formerly available rather than an exclusive claim to truth. Out of his concern with avoiding the "irrationalist fallacy,"[30] whereby it is held that when legal problems are not settled with logic they must have been settled arbitrarily, Gottlieb develops an important model of judicial decision.

Roberto Unger, though his work is grander in scope than Gottlieb's, approaches law from a perspective that is highly influenced by attention to language as a measure of the nature of legal action.[31] He uses linguistics to demonstrate the extent to which societies operate on schemes of classification which depict their existence.[32] These schemes form the common meanings that are the basis of action. It is a basis, he points out, that is least understood where there is an explicit normative component of the action,[33] as in research on law. Yet, here it is all the more important to employ "meaning" as a prism for viewing action,[34] in order to show "the sense an act makes against the background of a social code of rules, practices, and beliefs."[35]

In *Constitutional Bricolage*,[36] Gerald Garvey employs language as a metaphor to indicate the structural constraints that operate on judges because they have limited tools of the craftsman or "bricoleur." Although his debt is primarily to Levi-Strauss and the insights of structural anthropology, Garvey sees the process by which a culture achieves coherence as akin to the process by which different parts of speech are organized in sentences. Thus, he argues that "identification of the society's 'syntactical' principle furnishes a key to its constitutional processes."[37] According to this formulation, constitutional continuity is a reflection of the "deeper cultural unity" which he sees in a "buyer-seller" pattern of interactions.[38] The notion that the work of the Supreme Court Justices is limited by the cultural forms available is the most immediate contribution of Garvey's investigation to the present work. However, in the discussion of constitutional law as a language presented here, the claim is both that constitutional language operates on the basis of different forms from those of the society generally and that these forms are manipulated as a language. The particular linguistic processes that characterize the judicial decision are the key to the use of language.

Stuart Scheingold's work focuses on the acquired ways of proceeding that lawyers bring to their professional tasks.[39] Although his discussion concentrates on the roles that are more akin to rule-following than to linguistic activity, it is sympathetic to the significance of legal symbols for judicial creativity. Here, the "internal logic" of the rules is a key to professional certification which poses a constraint on legal action. The rule-mongering[40] that Scheingold sees as the result of legal training is thus based on experience. The legal grounds which the lawyer learns to offer and which the judge requires follow familiar conceptual patterns. Still more closely tied to the model of language is Richard Flathman's analysis of rights as "practices"—the conceptual bases of language which are discussed in the following chapters.[41] Flathman demonstrates the utility of language philosophy as a new perspective on social phenomena revealing rights as "patterns of thought and action."[42] His account establishes an epistemological basis for treating law as a form of social meaning which is best understood by research grounded in the way meaning operates.

Other recent work demonstrates the perception that language in law must be understood if the legal process is to be integrated into modern conceptions of epistemological issues. The casebook by Bishin and Stone[43] takes this approach, and a full statement is available in Walter Probert's work.[44] In addition, some empirical investigations by linguists and lawyers are likely to begin producing interesting results in the next few years.[45]

For the last thirty years, "judicial behavioralists" have attempted to describe what causes judges to behave as they do. As a reaction to the prescriptive concerns of traditional legal scholarship, two generations of scholars turned from legal doctrine to the matter of how judges respond to situations that reach them. The initial insights of C. Herman Pritchett[46] establishes the relevance of how the judge voted as a key to showing the political dimensions of the decision. Subsequent work, though elaborate in its methodological trappings, has not gone far beyond these initial insights. It has failed to broaden our understanding of judicial decision relative to other forms of political action, since its attention has been to a commonality between judges and other participants in the legal network.

The dominance of the tradition poses a challenge for those who would take on the unanswered question about judicial decision, especially with regard to those aspects which are unique. Is the political action that judges engage in different from that of other actors? We cannot fully understand judicial action within the framework of behavioral jurisprudence. Understanding is to be found in attention to the symbolic structure of communication that characterizes the judicial process, i.e., the concepts through which the judges interpret the world.

In his early work, Pritchett demonstrated a greater compatibility with the study of the symbolic parameters in law than subsequent behavioral developments would suggest. Rather than proposing that the uniqueness of the judiciary rests in an impartial adherence to precedent, Pritchett proposed that "the individual judge may think that the precedents are wrong or outmoded. . . . He is not free to ignore the precedents, to act as though they did not exist. He has free choice, but among limited alternatives."[47] Judicial action must acknowledge what has gone before, particularly if the judge chooses to make new law. Both choice and its subsequent explanation are a response to a world already symbolized. Judicial choice is limited because it must be intelligible. Judges cannot ignore the grammar of constitutional law, since it is by acquiring a unique conceptual background that they come to understand the Constitution and the issues presented to them.

In explaining decisions on appeal to the Constitution, the Justices of the Supreme Court employ a unique body of concepts derived from experience with the Constitution. The use of these concepts is also evident in legal briefs, oral arguments, and law review commentary, to cite only the public sources. The tradition constitutes a unique language, at least insofar as understanding it requires considerable experience. The thesis elaborated in the following pages applies theories of language to an area of investigation which has been dominated by social scientists. As a result of the orientation of past research to either norms or behavior, the manner in which linguistic experience functions in constitutional interpretation has not been adequately demonstrated. The approach developed here resists the choice between one or the other. I have attempted to show that the theory evident in ordinary language philosophy, and to a lesser extent in linguistics, suggests a new approach to the study of judicial action in that it reconsiders some basic premises about symbolic processes.

One source of insight for this study is the idea that native speakers of English do not say things like "red is industrious,"[48] "colorless green ideas sleep furiously,"[49] or "bring Thursday."[50] A basic premise of this study is that the same kind of constraint operates on the Justices of the Supreme Court when they decide a constitutional issue. That is, they are not likely to hold that "equal protection prohibits unreasonable searches," since this formulation is beyond the sensible options from which they must choose.

Because law operates as an authoritative-formal language for most citizens and as a professional-formal language for lawyers, this study of the judicial decision as "ordinary" language concentrates on the Supreme Court. Although these other spheres, since they employ systems of related symbols, can be better understood by attention to properties of language, the Justices of the Supreme Court are in a unique position. Their interpretation of the Constitution is not governed by the same system of authority that operates on ordinary citizens. Indeed, they use the constitutional tradition much as the ordinary citizens uses language. Because the thesis is unusual, I have sought to develop the nature of language, law, and the judicial decision concurrently.

This work begins with a discussion of the nature of words because apparently we first think of words when we think of a language. Thus, Chapter 2 considers the limitations of the empiricist position on the nature of words and discusses some contextual properties of the words in the Constitution. Chapter 3 examines behavioral studies of the judicial decision to show the limits of positivist explanations. For words to be considered a language, even in the traditional sense of what constitutes a language, there must be structural properties for the way the words are used. Chapter 4 analyzes the structures that are evident in the sentences in the Constitution and suggests that the organization of these words can be investigated in order to point out how language shows what is meant in the document. These chapters lay the foundation for the relevance of linguistic analysis to the study of constitutional interpretation.

Chapter 5 expands some of the principles of a theory or model of language derived from ordinary language philosophy. Special attention is paid to aspects of this theory of language which reveal why it is a source of some interesting insights into constitutional law. Chapter 6 demonstrates why constitutional law can itself be considered a language. The chapter considers the language of the Constitution and theories about how languages operate. It proposes that constitutional law consists of certain practices which are revealed by the grammar used in constitutional adjudication.

The interpretive or creative aspects of language are developed in Chapter 7, with reference to judicial decision-making. Language acquisition is related to the learning of law, and the process of "going on" in a new context in language is shown to be similar to the process of judicial interpretation. In Chapter 8, sense and criteria in the use of concepts are discussed and the constitutional right of privacy is examined for what its use reveals about the judi-

cial decision. The final chapter proposes that, at the level of constitutional decision by the Supreme Court, the finality of the Court
makes decision in this sphere much more akin to the ordinary use
of language than to action governed by rule. This is the basis for an
analysis of the nature of legal authority as it is manifested in the
substance of the constitutional tradition.

NOTES

1. Harold Lasswell, *Politics, Who Gets What, When, How* (New York,
1936).
2. Thurman Arnold, *The Symbols of Government* (New Haven: Yale
University Press, 1935).
3. Murray Edelman, *The Symbolic Uses of Politics* (Urbana, Ill.:
University of Illinois Press, 1964), p. 5.
4. Peter Berger and Thomas Luckmann, *The Social Construction of
Reality* (New York: Doubleday, 1966); Kenneth Boulding, *The Image*
(Ann Arbor, Mich.: University of Michigan Press, 1965); Herbert Marcuse, *One-Dimensional Man* (Boston: Beacon Press, 1964).
5. Frances F. Piven and Richard A. Cloward, *Regulating the Poor*
(New York: Pantheon, 1971).
6. Murray Edelman, *Politics as Symbolic Action: Mass Arousal and
Quiescence* (New York: Academic Press, 1971).
7. Hannah Pitkin, *Wittgenstein and Justice* (Berkeley: University of
California Press, 1972); Richard E. Flathman, *Political Obligation* (New
York: Atheneum, 1972).
8. Peter Winch, *The Idea of a Social Science* (London: Routledge and
Kegan Paul, 1958); Harold Garfinkel, *Studies in Ethnomethodology*
(Englewood Cliffs, N.J.: Prentice-Hall, 1967); John Gunnell, *Philosophy,
Science and Political Inquiry* (Morristown, N.J.: General Learning Press,
1975).
9. Winch, op. cit., pp. 11-12.
10. Ibid.
11. Ibid., p. 15.
12. Charles Taylor, "Interpretation and the Sciences of Man," *Review
of Metaphysics* (September 1971).
13. Gunnell, op. cit., p. v.
14. Ibid., Chapter 6.
15. Ibid., p. 246.
16. Robin Lakoff, *Language and Woman's Place* (New York: Harper
and Row, 1975).

17. Murray Edelman, *Political Language* (New York: Academic Press, 1977).

18. Ibid., p. 23.

19. Claus Mueller, *The Politics of Communication* (London: Oxford University Press, 1973).

20. William E. Connolly, *The Terms of Political Discourse* (Lexington, Mass.: D. C. Heath, 1974).

21. Mueller, op. cit., p. 13.

22. Ibid.

23. Connolly, op. cit., p. 3.

24. H.L.A. Hart, "Definition and Theory in Jurisprudence," *Law Quarterly Review* 37 (1954):70; for a related view, see Lon Fuller, *Legal Fictions* (Stanford, Calif.: Stanford University Press, 1967).

25. H.L.A. Hart, *The Concept of Law* (New York: Oxford University Press, 1960).

26. Ronald Dworkin, *Taking Rights Seriously* (Cambridge, Mass.: Harvard University Press, 1976).

27. Gidon Gottlieb, *The Logic of Choice* (London: Allen and Unwin, 1968).

28. See also Stephen Toulmin, *The Uses of Argument* (Cambridge: Cambridge University Press, 1964); Chaim Perelman, *The Idea of Justice and the Problem of Argument* (New York: Humanities Press, 1963); Rolf Sartorius, "The Justification of the Judicial Decision," *Ethics* 78 (1968): 171; J. C. Smith, "Law, Language, and Philosophy," *University of British Columbia Law Review* (May 1968):59.

29. Gottlieb, op. cit., p. 21.

30. Richard Wasserstrom, *The Judicial Decision* (Stanford: Stanford University Press, 1961), p. 23.

31. Roberto Unger, *Law in Modern Society* (New York: Free Press, 1976).

32. Ibid., pp. 251-252.

33. Ibid., p. 245.

34. Ibid., p. 248.

35. Ibid., p. 254.

36. Gerald Garvey, *Constitutional Bricolage* (Princeton, N.J.: Princeton University Press, 1971).

37. Ibid., p. 3.

38. Ibid., p. 4.

39. Stuart Scheingold, *The Politics of Rights* (New Haven, Conn.: Yale University Press, 1974).

40. Ibid., p. 152.

41. Richard Flathman, *The Practice of Rights* (Cambridge: Cambridge University Press, 1977).

42. Ibid., p. 1.

43. William R. Bishin and Christopher Stone, *Law, Language and Ethics* (Mineola, N.Y.: Foundation Press, 1972). See also Ovid C. Lewis, et al., "Symposium: Law, Language and Communication," *Case Western Reserve Law Review* 23 (Winter 1972):307.

44. Walter Probert, *Law, Language and Communication* (Springfield, Ill.: Charles C. Thomas, 1972); "Law Through the Looking Glass of Language and Communication Behavior," *Journal of Legal Education* 3 (1968):20.

45. Brenda Danet, "The Role of Language in the Legal Process" (NSF Grant, 1975). See also the work of the Institute for Applied Linguistics, Washington, D.C.

46. C. Herman Pritchett, *The Roosevelt Court: A Study in Judicial Politics and Values, 1937–1947* (New York: Macmillan Co., 1948).

47. C. Herman Pritchett, *Civil Liberties and the Vinson Court* (Chicago: University of Chicago Press, 1954), p. 187.

48. Frederick Waismann, *Principles of Linguistic Philosophy* (London: Macmillan, 1965).

49. Noam Chomsky, *Aspects of a Theory of Syntax* (Cambridge, Mass.: M.I.T. Press, 1965).

50. Bernard Harrison, *Meaning and Structure: An Essay in the Philosophy of Language* (New York: Harper and Row, 1972).

2 | Words in the Constitution

While the Constitution is more than just words, the words are important, constituting the preeminent political lexicon in the American language. Moreover, the way they have come to be used by the Justices of the Supreme Court has a bearing on American politics. Many of the contests in American politics are carried out through litigation where the authoritative decision is made by this Court. Investigating the meaning of the words in this document is the first step in describing how language influences judicial decision. As used by the Justices, words in the Constitution have the linguistic qualities which give meaning to discourse in ordinary language. The meaning of words in this realm is the basis for judicial decision. The decision itself, as a choice between possible meanings, delineates what forms of political action are to receive the sanction of the state. The shared meanings that comprise the framework for authoritative decision reveal the parameters of American political life.

Students of the Constitution are familiar with the way words like "commerce," "equal protection," and "jury" have been interpreted by the Supreme Court. Such interpretations invariably rely on the "meaning" of the words. This chapter discusses the limitations of a predominant view of language and suggests the contributions of modern linguistic theory to overcoming these limitations. An effort is made to point out the significance of formal definition in the Constitution as compared with the particular spheres of activity from which different words in the Constitution are taken. This effort relies on students of language rather than on students of law or the Constitution. Thus, I shall refer to the philosophy of language and to linguistic theory in order to lay the foundation for a discussion of sources of meaning for the words in the Constitution.

As mentioned earlier, when we think of language, we usually think first of words. It is thus instructive to introduce the study of constitutional language with a consideration of semantics, the study of words and their meaning. Partly because the meaning of words has been the focus of so much of linguistic theory, it is a good basis for exploring traditional views on language. One goal of this study is to demonstrate these views and their effect on understanding the judicial decision. Hence, we begin with words in order to show that their meaning cannot be established independently of their place in a language. It is a proper beginning because it reveals a fallacy in traditional approaches to judicial decision.

Constitutional law posits many theories on the proper sources for the meaning of the words in the document. Two positions, however, cover the range of conventionally accepted possibilities: the meaning is either fixed in the time the document was written, or it may change with subsequent perception. W. W. Crosskey maintains that the intent of the framers ought to be the basis of a proper understanding of the meaning of the words in the Constitution.[1] His scholarship documents the original meanings of the words. Implicit in his discussion is the recognition that word meanings have a contextual base, but that the base remains constant. This position lends support to Justice Burger's opinion in the death penalty case, *Furman v. Georgia* (1972).[2] In his evaluation of the meaning of the Eighth Amendment's ban on "cruel and unusual punishments," Burger stated that "if the Constitution proscribed every punishment producing severe emotional stress, then capital punishment would clearly have been impermissible in 1791." In this view, Burger is already moving somewhat from the polar position adhered to by Crosskey, but this is not going so far as others would in allowing interpretations of the document to simply be a product of experience. Thus, in his majority opinion in a subsequent death penalty case, *Gregg v. Georgia* (1976),[3] Justice Stewart relied on the view that "a principle to be vital must be capable of wider application than the mischief which gave it birth," which he took from *Weems v. United States* (1910).[4] This approach has been called "experiential"[5] since it emphasizes the importance of the existing social and political context within which any definition is made. Both the intent of the framers and contemporary social life constitute experiential bases for the meaning of the words in the Constitution. Modern conceptions of language lend support to the more flexible social interpretation of meaning, since the intent of the framers in the context of the law is a stipulation that explicitly seeks to stop the evolution of meaning. In this sense, the discussion in the following pages cannot (nor does it seek to) set a standard for constitutional interpretation. Instead, the view here is that a discussion of the nature of language may clarify the capacity of students of politics to describe the process of interpretation rather than enter into that process with a perception of the appropriate sources of meaning. Toward this end, it is reasonable to begin with the epistemological constraints that have traditionally inhibited a full and adequate treatment of the process of constitutional interpretation.

THE EMPIRICIST THEORY OF LANGUAGE

The nature of language has always had a significant place in the study of meaning. The predominant view among philosophers who have influenced the social sciences has been that the essence of language exists in a relation between words and the objects to which they refer. This position, the positivist or empiricist theory of language,[6] inadequately describes some essential features of ordinary language which have considerable bearing on judicial decision in a realm like constitutional law, which has many of these features. Some elaboration of the theory is necessary in order to show its appeal and to provide a foundation for a discussion of its inadequacies.

In determining the relation between language and the world, the empiricist position distinguishes between facts in the world and the language through which they are represented. It describes language as being composed of words representing facts. The words are arranged in propositions which express valuations, but the words have an empirical base. The structure or logic of language is in how words are put together. This logic, though prescribing how we ought to speak, is supposed to reflect or portray a logic that is in the world. There is thus a distinction between the factual world and how it is depicted. This theory is associated with Bertrand Russell and the early work of Ludwig Wittgenstein.[7]

According to this theory, the objects in the world are given "names" which signify the objects. The meaning of words is completely contained in the objects they represent.[8] In this sense, if there is no object that a name signifies, it is meaningless.[9] Words that seem to have this quality can be seen in the Constitution. The Constitution was, of course, a blueprint before it became a description of the institutional structure of American politics. As such, before it was put into practice, it identified "things," like Senators, Electors, and a House of Representatives, that did not exist. As a result, there is a continuing sense that the process of putting a scheme into practice determines in part the nature of the constitutional construct. The initial discussion of the blueprint, its acceptability, and subsequent treatment of these words were based on the perception that the words referred to something known that could become something real.

In this theory, the meaning of the symbol, or word, is found by reference to the object. According to Wittgenstein, "every word has a meaning. This meaning is correlated with the word. It is the object for which the word stands."[10] Wittgenstein is here summarizing the empiricist position as he finds it expressed by Saint Augustine. This position suggests that the acquisition of language must ultimately be based on ostensive definition. A classic statement of ostensive definition comes from Saint Augustine: " . . . as I heard words repeatedly used in their proper places in various sentences, I gradually learnt to understand what objects they signified. . . ."[11] Ostensive definition is the keystone of the empiricist theory because it is "the only explanation which can work without any previous knowledge . . . . We conclude that there is no way of understanding any meaning without ultimate reference to ostensive definition."[12]

According to this theory, the concepts which allow the words to be used are usually related to the process of inductive generalization. To acquire a concept in language, one must learn to recognize "the members of the class of objects, events, states of affairs, and so on" as having a symbol which stands for the concept.[13] The theories of verification and inductive generalization exemplify the correlation between the empiricist theory and scientific positivism. These formulations have been the basis for theories of the acquisition and use of language in the behavioral sciences.[14] In behavioral psychology, the attempt to explain the functions of symbols on the basis of the stimulus-response model operates within this conceptual framework.[15] The associative-referential theory of meaning is fundamental to psychological theories of verbal behavior based on a stimulus-response mechanism.

Of all the words in the Constitution, the Bill of Rights, and the Amendments, the following are some of the most important. Yet, their meaning has presented little difficulty for judicial decision.

United States of America
President
Congress
House of Representatives and Senate
Supreme Court
Senator
Representative
Chief Justice

These "Constitution words" are defined in the document, and like the ordinary words that define them, they have not been the subject of extensive judicial interpretation. The "United States of America" provides one of the best illustrations of these words. This string of words in the Constitution is a specific reference clearly dependent on the constitutional formulation. In the case of "United States of America," as with all similar words, it took more than the Constitution to give them the significance they now have. Without their use in the Constitution, however, the subsequent developments which gave the present meaning to these words would not have been possible.

The words "Congress," "Senate," "House of Representatives," and "Supreme Court" all have, I believe, the same semantic status as "United States." That is, like "United States," these words depend on usage in the Constitution for the meaning accorded to them in constitutional law. They have come to have their meaning for students of the Constitution because of what is said about them in the document. All of these words have important connotations that facilitated the acquisition of their meaning. However, the document contains a good deal more information about the meaning of these words than is available for many of the other important words in the Constitution. Consequently, these words are less subject to problems of interpretation than those which depend on different contexts for their explanation.

By way of example, an unknown may be substituted for any of those words in order to consider the possibilities and limitations that result. If "X" is substituted for the word "Senate" throughout the document, we can still make sense out of a sentence such as the following, since the document further elaborates what a Senate is. "All legislative Powers herein granted shall be vested in a Congress of the United States, which shall consist of an 'X' and a House of Representatives." We come to know what an "X" is when the document subsequently states that "the 'X' of the United States shall be composed of two Senators from each state." The word "Senator" is further explained in terms of its functions.

The fact that such substitutions can be made and the words can still retain their meaning is indicative of the degree to which the meaning of these words is a matter of the document's construction. That some words are susceptible to such substitution is not meant to suggest that they do not bring to the document some clues to their meaning. Since the etymology of words such as "Senator" or "Congress" is quite long, the traditional understandings have given depth even to words which are by and large sufficiently defined in the document for their meaning to be clear. The original meaning of "Senator" gives us the clues to what sort of thing it is which allows us to carry it along until it is more fully defined. Because of the elaboration in the document, the original meanings may be superseded in the constitutional context.

Because of the elaboration in the Constitution, the determination of meaning has in some cases been easy. Interpretation of these words is almost mechanical in the idealized sense that had been used to characterize the judicial decision in the past. In the Constitution, however, the meaning of many words lies beyond the relatively clear boundaries of the formal constructs. The utility of modern linguistic analysis is that it deals primarily with interpretations which transcend the boundaries of the formal constructs.

The state of affairs that exists with propositions is central to the empiricist theory and provides the framework for the word-object relation. It is mentioned here because the treatment of the structure of language by the empiricist theory has been the basis for the orientation of judicial decision and the interpretation of that decision. Legal propositions express valuations which are related to the constitutional world as logic is to reason for a logician. Thus, in *Furman*,[16] Justice Stewart in his majority opinion declared that the contention that the Georgia statute violated the Constitution was false. This is a structural element of the decision that each Justice adheres to and that gives the impression that the empiricist position adequately portrays their activity—which, of course, is what it is supposed to do.

Since propositions in the empiricist theory are composed of elements that represent basic facts, they depict the world as a picture. The "picture theory" is one of Wittgenstein's early contributions to the study of meaning in language.[17] He considered propositions to be like pictures in that they represent the world.[18] Propositions in language not only represent objects that exist; what the picture depicts may be imaginary. What is crucial to the theory is that if a picture depicts a state of affairs that does not exist, the picture can be shown to be false.[19] This certainty is the basis for the orientation and tenor of constitutional interpretation. Constitutional statements such as "All legislative Powers herein granted shall be vested in a Congress of the United States . . . " represent such propositional statements. They depict a political state of affairs, and the extent to which they are accurate representations can be examined in terms of the truth or falsity of the propositions. Indeed, much constitutional politics revolves around the extent to which current practice is perceived to be in accord with constitutional statements. When the Supreme Court appears to be legislating, it is with reference to the meaning of these statements.

Thus, the epistemological position of the empiricist theory proposes a correlation between word and thing and limits propositions to those which can be determined to be true or false by comparison with the world. This stance is at the root of behavioralism in general. In behavioral theories of language, words are taken to be the response to factual stimuli. B. F. Skinner, for example, proposes a functional analysis of verbal behavior. He describes variables as controlling the acquisition and use of language and specifies how they interact to determine a specific verbal response. The variables are factors which have been developed in the study of animal behavior, such as stimulus, reinforcement, and deprivation. This discussion of the nature of language serves as an example of the relation of the empiricist theory to the behavioral position.[20]

In the theory of language acquisition and use in terms of ostensive definition, the manner in which we acquire the name of an object is essentially the same as Skinner's account of learning language in terms of learning the basic linguistic elements—"tacts."[21] In the Skinnerian model, a "tact" is associated with an object, quality, or activity through conditioned behavior. It acquires its meaning by being associated with a repeated stimulus. A "tact" may be compared to a "name" in the theory just discussed. The naming operation is central to both theories. Since "tacts" and "names" have the same reference and are acquired in the same way, behavioral theories and those of positivism in philosophy have the same epistemological foundation.

There are a number of other contemporary psychological theories of language which diverge from Skinner's position in some respects but support the claim that the empiricist theory has remained fundamental to the scientific investigation of symbolic processes.[22] These theories retain the position that meaning must be understood as some sort of relation between the linguistic symbol and the thing symbolized, and that the symbols are somehow organized for the speaker as a result of the nature of what is symbolized. Even mediation theories such as those of O. Hobart Mowrer, which diverge significantly from behavioralism, retain the basic word-object dichotomy. Unlike modern linguistics, Mowrer "fails to explain the nature of the connection between the mediating responses which according to (his theory) constitute the meaning of words and sentences and the overt behavioral and verbal responses which actually manifest someone's understanding of an utterance in the language he knows."[23] Ultimately, he must appeal to the central principle of the empiricist theory, that know-

In an article by Saul Cohen discussing Justice Holmes's position on copyright law, the affinity between the position of the realists and the general semanticists is evident. Cohen praises Holmes for recognizing that experience gives insight into the way words will be used.[32] But the highest praise is accorded to Holmes's recognition that words are merely labels and that there are underlying realities that language does not reveal. Language, according to this analysis, is an imperfect tool in the attempt to represent the world accurately.

From this tenet in the semanticist's position, we get the emphasis on the flexibility and plasticity of words. Holmes stated the position in a 1918 opinion: "A word is not a crystal, transparent and unchanged, it is the skin of a living thought and may vary greatly in color and content according to the circumstances and the time in which it is used."[33] Both legal realists and general semanticists maintain that legal language needs semantic therapy. Little is positively credited to legal language. Its imperfections are to be avoided by turning from abstractions to reality. This point is more clearly established by another statement from the highly quotable Justice Holmes. "We must think things not words, or at least we must constantly translate our words into the facts for which they stand, if we are to keep to the real and the true."[34] Some who would follow Holmes in other respects have found this position unrealistic. Where the translation into facts is held to be too much to expect, we are cautioned at least to recognize that legal language is not the ideal tool that it might be. Even the pragmatic position contains a warning grounded in the empiricist theory.

In *The Tyranny of Words*, Stuart Chase devoted a chapter to the issue of deriving meaning from the Constitution.[35] His concern was about the highly abstract nature of words in the Constitution or what he called the "weasel words in the jargon of lawyers." He stated that the words were more emotionally charged than they had to be. According to Chase, the problem with legal language lay in the fact that it was too abstract, by which he meant that it had no clear referents: "There is no certainty, no surety, no omniscience in the law except in ghostly realms."[36] The solution Chase proposed was to direct the judges to the "real" world outside themselves and away from the "unreal" verbiage they had created and preserved.

The analysis of legal language on the basis of the empiricist theory has concentrated on the advocacy of precision. It has painted a dreary picture of the influence of language in law, suggesting that legal language has been an impediment to the ideal of precision. The following discussion lays the foundation for a more affirmative evaluation of this influence. It suggests that the way language operates can tell the student of law a good deal more about judicial interpretation than those tied to the empiricist theory have been able to discern.

GIVING WORDS THEIR DUE

A modern linguistic perspective on the meaning of words shows the limitations of the approaches which have been derived from the empiricist position. Recent developments in the study of language, which have come from structural linguistics and ordinary language philosophy, challenge the empiricist theory of meaning on the basis of the claimed word-object relationship and the account of language learning by ostensive definition. These theories, and the psycholinguistic research which they have stimulated, suggest the utility of this approach to legal behavior. They transcend the limitations traditionally placed on our theoretical framework as a consequence of the positivistic epistemology which has been fundamental to social-scientific research. These developments demonstrate that certain competencies are essential to learning language and hence must be considered basic to language itself. I shall briefly consider some of the elements of the modern linguistic critique of the empiricist theory. These factors comprise the grounds for a reexamination of the words in the Constitution as an element in judicial decision that eliminates the legal mythology of mechanical jurisprudence without ignoring the substance of the law.

The linguists in the tradition of Noam Chomsky have proposed that the associationist account fails to consider what they believe to be a facet of language, namely, that intelligent use depends at least in part on internal structures which comprise linguistic competence.

For Chomsky, these structures are the source of the grammatical expressions of a language.[37] Chomsky has specifically directed his attack toward the behavioralist position.[38]

For Ludwig Wittgenstein and ordinary language philosophy, the attack begins with a criticism of the theory of ostensive definition. This position argues that pointing to an object as a ground for the definition of a word can only work as a source of language acquisition if the learner already understands something about the meaning of the pointing gesture and the function of the word in language. The learner must know when a sound is being defined and have some context to which the definition may be attached. Such a stance parallels Chomsky's position in suggesting that an adult's use of language depends not just on the basic associations of the behavioral model but more fundamentally on a system of linguistic competencies.

The critique of Saint Augustine's formulation of language learning points out the limits of ostensive definition as a basis for the description of the essence of language. Wittgenstein suggests that "Augustine describes the learning of human language as if the child came into a strange country and did not understand the language of the country; that is, as if it already had a language, only not this one."[39] Thus, Wittgenstein's position is that ostensive definition may describe how we come to know some words once we have mastered the fundamentals of language that enable us to make sense out of the definitions, i.e., that enable us to know how the definition is to be taken. In this regard, certain concepts and linguistic practices are basic to the understanding of ostensive definition.

The operation of these concepts for the Justices suggests the importance of attention to the process of learning the law which is one of the dimensions of constitutional language investigated subsequently (Chapter 7). It is acknowledged here that the process depends first on the acquisition of English and secondarily on the vocabulary and grammar of the Constitution which is itself deeply embedded in the larger legal context. It is the secondary characteristics that are the most significant for the political activity of constitutional interpretation, although the political significance of language in general has been receiving increasing attention.[40] In this context, the acquisition of particular words in the constitutional setting depends on mastery of the context in which they are used. It requires attention to the relevant structure that gives them meaning. Words like "due process" and "interstate commerce" are classic examples.

Modern empiricists, such as W.V.O. Quine, have proposed a modified "empiricist theory"[41] which eliminates some of the problems that result from the development of a theory of language from the correlation of word and object.

To give the meaning of a proposition is, (for Quine), in the end, to use it, or some other logically connected proposition, to assert some truth: the system of meanings and the system of true empirical propositions in their full array of logical and theoretical connections (the "field of total science") are in the end, for Quine, coextensive.[42]

Harrison finds Quine's position wanting in its capacity to account for the use of language in novel situations. According to this criticism, Quine fails to explain linguistic creativity because there is a gap in his theory between observed regularity and prescriptive rules. Harrison argues that the Quinean account fails to explain "how the learner translates an array of circumstantial observations about the behavior of others, into a set of rules for his performances."[43] Harrison's account, which integrates the position of both Chomsky and Wittgenstein, proposes that it is possible to state the meaning of any sentence in a language without saying anything about the truth of statements in that language, simply by reference to a finite system of linguistic rules.

An initial step in giving words their due in judicial decision on the Constitution is to delineate the rich traditions that the various controversial words in the Constitution have. The words in the Constitution reflect the formal qualities characteristic of a subset of legal discourse. In this sense, some of the words in the Constitution derive their meaning from the structural relations enunciated in the document. One of the most important functions of the Constitution has been to establish bodies, offices, and procedures for operating a system of government. The framework for what these bodies, offices, and procedures were supposed to be like is laid out in the definitions of these words in the document. Words whose meaning is determined by construction in the document can be called "Constitution words." These have already been discussed as representative of the sort of words that the empiricist theory best accounts for.

The words in the Constitution that initially derive their meaning from use "outside" this setting include a different type of words than those discussed so far. Although not all the other words in the Constitution merit consideration, they all influence interpretation to some degree because of the importance of the linguistic context in the determination of meaning (to be explored further in Chapter 4).

Two subclasses of these "extra" Constitution words are proposed here in order to emphasize the importance of use and context for their meaning. Both subclasses demonstrate problems of meaning and definition which transcend the document. Subclass (1) consists of the ordinary English words that enable the elaboration of the constitutional scheme. Subclass (2) comprises those words whose meaning is derived from a more specialized activity with which they have been readily associated. Such usage has considerable bearing on the development and determination of meaning, and for many words in the Constitution it is specialized or technical enough to be distinguishable from ordinary English.

(1) Words such as "punish," "commerce," and "religion" bring to the Constitution their own set of conventions. Although this is also true of those words defined in the document, in the case of these words, ordinary usage assumes greater significance as an influence on the determination of meaning. The meaning at the time of the Constitutional Convention, as well as the usage in the Convention itself, may influence any determination of the meaning of these words. Or, it may be experience that suggests how these words are to be taken. An argument as to the proper source of interpretive criteria is part of the politics of the Constitution. Here, in considering the linguistic aspects of the Constitution, it is important to demonstrate simply that the meaning of some words

emerges from the way we have come to use them. The argument as to whether tradition or experience should be the source of meaning is one of jurisprudential interest, as has already been suggested. The student of constitutional law knows many of the words in the document before he can (or is likely to) have the chance to learn the specialized development of constitutional interpretation. In the study of the Constitution, some words acquire a new depth and greater influence than they had prior to their use in the Constitution. But these are still "words" whether they are learned in childhood or in the study of constitutional law. Hence, the use of the ordinary words in the Constitution can be explained in terms of the principles of ordinary language use, and the interpretation of the Constitution can be viewed as dependent on those principles.

The subclass (2) of extra Constitution words consists of those that come directly from a particular sphere of human activity and are used by those engaged in the activity. Because of this use, they are semantically tied to an extra-constitutional base. The predominant example of such an activity in the Constitution is legal. Law has its own technical vocabulary and also uses ordinary language in a special way. Many crucial words in the Constitution derive their meaning from the legal tradition.

The technical vocabulary of law used in the Constitution is composed of such words as "indictment," "jury," "trial," "case," "felony," and "Writ of Habeas Corpus." These technical words belong to legal practice and describe the unique practices, institutions, and processes that are peculiar to legal activity. Legal practice produces its own distinct vocabulary. When these words are also used in the Constitution, their meaning is necessarily influenced by the way they have come to be used by lawyers and judges. In Chapter 6, it is contended that the practices which these legal terms reveal, along with the unique practices of the Constitution, form the basis for the consideration of constitutional law as a language.

The law also uses ordinary English, but in a special way. The specialized vocabulary of law evident in the Constitution includes words such as "judgment," "offense," "jurisdiction," "witness," and "probable cause."[44] Ordinary English changes when it is constantly put to the unique tests that exist in law. The specialized usage of law is the product of the particular practices and the unique tradition that have produced technical words and have used English in a special way. This usage has been called a "superimposed variation or argot."[45] These words, when interpreted in the Constitution, depend to some degree for their meaning on the tradition in law of the special use to which these English words have been put.

Politics also contributes special usages to the Constitution, although not nearly as obviously as law has. Words such as "Republican form of Government," "Bill of attainder," "ballot," or even "state legislature" rely for their meaning on a tradition of political activity. Like other activities, politics has its own unique terms. Some words are merely distinctive ways of referring to general activities. Those suggested here, however, represent unique practices of political life. Their influence in the Constitution suggests another dimension to constitutional language. The words in the Constitution that come from other spheres of activity cannot escape the influence of those activities on their meaning. To understand these words, one must to some degree rely on the situations in which they are ordinarily used.

It is the richness of this new attention to language and its capacity to handle the use of language in novel situations that makes it so attractive for the study of constitutional interpretation. Again, it certainly has other applications in the study of law, as perhaps in the case of a trial judge's decision as to whether a particular bit of testimony is hearsay, but it is in constitutional interpretation that the assessment of new situations by the Justices has the authoritative significance of stating the society's way of proceeding. Each petition for review, each hearing on merits in the Supreme Court, is new in this sense. It takes a situation and addresses it in terms of its accordance with the tradition of understanding that may presume to cover it.

Although linguists and ordinary language philosophers disagree strongly on some aspects of language, they are united in their opposition to the empiricist theory.[46] Much of the criticism of the philosophical approach leveled by linguists is directed toward the methodological limits of philosophical investigations. In reacting to this criticism, Harrison has taken the philosophical position of

Wittgenstein and has combined it with the more developed analytical devices of linguistics. The importance of this synthesis is
great, since the criticism from linguistics is based largely on a concern for a lack of rigor among the philosophers and does not consider a union such as Harrison has proposed. The development of
operational rules, which Harrison proposes, is based on the generative or transformational grammar of Chomsky and his partisans.
While such rules may tell us much about the use of language in law,
particularly about the application of legal words and concepts to
new cases, an application of these rules is beyond the scope of this
work. Indeed, it would be a diversion from the fundamentals of the
enterprise.[47]

Given the current orientation of social scientists, the relation
between language and constitutional law is most meaningful. This
relation can demonstrate the operation of symbolic processes that
enable and constrain, and that portray the world at the same time
that they limit what can be said about it. A certain rigor might
ultimately be sought in order to demonstrate the power of the
method of linguistics and to convey the uniqueness of its perspective. In introducing the relationship between a stance on
language and a traditionally rule-governed sphere, however, the
danger of seeing formal structural analysis in the Constitution is
that it could be interpreted as a statement of acceptable use of the
law rather than conventional use, which is the descriptive goal here.
It is more dramatic at this point to claim that conceptual structures operate in the law independent of rules than it is to provide a
formal "structural description" which cannot help but look like
rules, until the description of constitutional language has been
established.

Through exploration of the critique of the empiricist position in
terms of modern linguistic theory, it has been suggested that the
words that constitute the basis for judicial decision acquire their
meaning through use. The groups of words considered here, with
their varied sources of meaning, all contribute to the language of
the Constitution. These words, united in the document, constitute the means of communicating particular concepts and ideas. As
is made clearer subsequently, the distinction of words from their

context is an artificial one. I have begun with the consideration of individual words in order to demonstrate the importance of context and the limits of "realist" as well as traditional approaches to meaning in law. The next chapter relates contemporary behavioralist studies to this tradition and suggests the significance which an absence of attention to context has for the study of politics.

NOTES

1. W. W. Crosskey, *Politics and the Constitution in the History of the United States* (Chicago: University of Chicago Press, 1953).

2. 408 U.S. 238.

3. 428 U.S. 153.

4. 217 U.S. 349.

5. C. Herman Pritchett, *The American Constitution* (New York: McGraw-Hill, 1959), pp. 49–50.

6. Bernard Harrison, op. cit.

7. Ludwig Wittgenstein, *Tractatus Logico-Philosophicus,* translated by D. F. Pears and B. F. McGuiness with the Introduction by Bertrand Russell (London: Routledge and Kegan Paul, 1961).

8. Ibid., par. 3.22.

9. Ibid., par. 3.203.

10. Ludwig Wittgenstein, *Philosophical Investigations* (New York: Macmillan Co., 1958), par. 1.

11. Saint Augustine, *Confessions,* I.8.

12. Moritz Schlick, "Meaning and Verification," *Philosophical Review* 45 (1936):339–369.

13. Harrison, op. cit., p. 8.

14. Ibid., p. 5.

15. Ibid., p. 299.

16. 408 U.S. 238.

17. Wittgenstein, *Tractatus,* par. 2.1–3.05.

18. Ibid., par. 2.131.

19. Ibid., par. 2.21.

20. B. F. Skinner, *Verbal Behavior* (New York: Appleton-Century-Crofts, 1957).

21. Harrison, op. cit., p. 309.

22. C. E. Osgood, *Method and Theory in Experimental Psychology* (New York: Oxford University Press, 1953); O. Hobart Mowrer, *Learning Theory and the Symbolic Processes* (New York: John Wiley, 1960).

23. Harrison, op. cit., p. 307.

24. Ibid., p. 308.

25. David Mellinkoff, *The Language of the Law* (Boston: Little, Brown and Co., 1963).

26. Ibid., p. 294.

27. Frederick A. Philbrick, *Language and the Law* (New York: Macmillan Co., 1949).

28. Walter Probert, "Law and Persuasion: The Language Behavior of Lawyers," *University of Pennsylvania Law Review* 35 (1959): 108; Probert, "Symposium on Law, Language and Communication," *Western Reserve Law Review* 9 (1958): 115.

29. The following contain attacks on the legend of precision in the language of law, and most of them derive from positivism: Zechariah Chafee, "The Disorderly Conduct of Words," *Columbia Law Review* 41 (1941):381; Jerome Frank, *Law and the Modern Mind* (New York: Brentano's, 1930); Felix Cohen, "Transcendental Nonsense and the Functional Approach," *Columbia Law Review* 35 (1935):809; W. Wesley Hohfeld, "Some Fundamental Legal Conceptions as Applied in Judicial Reasoning," *Yale Law Journal* 23 (1913):16; *Guild Review* 14 (1954):138; Glanville Williams, "Language and the Law," *Law Quarterly Review* 61 (1945):71–86, 179–95, 293–303, 284–406.

30. Frederick K. Beutel, "Elementary Semantics: Critique of Realism and Experimental Jurisprudence," *Journal of Legal Education* 13 (1960): 67; see also Beutel, "The Relationship of Experimental Jurisprudence to Other Schools of Jurisprudence and the Scientific Method," *Washington University Law Quarterly* 71 (1971):385.

31. K. N. Llewellyn, *The Bramble Bush* (New York: Oceana Publications, 1951), p. 12. Emphasis mine.

32. Saul Cohen, "Justice Holmes and Copyright Law," *ETC.* 23 (December 1966):440.

33. *Towne v. Eisner*, 245 U.S. 418, 425 (1918).

34. Oliver Wendell Holmes, *Collected Legal Papers* (New York: Harcourt, Brace and Howe, 1920), p. 238.

35. Stuart Chase, *The Tyranny of Words* (New York: Harcourt, Brace and Co., 1939).

36. Ibid., p. 327.

37. Noam Chomsky, op. cit.

38. Noam Chomsky, "Review of *Verbal Behavior*," *Language* 35 (1958): 26–58.

39. Wittgenstein, *Philosophical Investigations*, par. 32.

40. See, for instance, Mueller, op. cit.

41. W.V.O. Quine, *Word and Object* (Cambridge, Mass.: M.I.T. Press, 1960).

42. Harrison, op. cit., p. 184.

43. Ibid., p. 82.

44. Mellinkoff, op. cit., p. 16.

45. Ovid C. Lewis, et al., op. cit., p. 314.

46. Jerry A. Fodor and Jerrold J. Katz, *The Structure of Language* (Englewood Cliffs, N.J.: Prentice-Hall, 1964); Jerrold J. Katz, *The Philosophy of Language* (New York: Harper and Row, 1966); Colin Lyas, *Philosophy and Linguistics* (London: Macmillan, 1971).

47. For a possible framework, see Chomsky, *Aspects of a Theory of Syntax.*

3 | Beyond the Behavioral Model of Judicial Decision

Analysis of constitutional interpretation on the basis of its linguistic characteristics suggests a new perspective on appellate judicial decision-making. The application of linguistic theory to judicial decision is related here to political research on the behavior of judges. As an introduction to this analysis, the traditional positivistic presumptions of social science are discussed in terms of theories of meaning in language in order to show the conceptual limitations that have affected research on judicial behavior. The particular claims of leading behavioralists are examined, and concern is expressed for their capacity to develop the uniquely legal dimensions of decision. Finally, an initial suggestion is made about the prospects for incorporating legal factors in the judicial decision where precedent does not govern the position taken.

This chapter concentrates on the attitudinal dimension evident in recent studies of judicial decision-making. (The transitional theory of the judicial role is considered in Chapter 5.) Selected works from Glendon Schubert, Sidney S. Ulmer, David W. Rohde, and Harold J. Spaeth are taken as representative of this approach.[1] In considering the contributions of these scholars, the focus is on the epistemological foundations of the psychological position evident in this school of thought, rather than on the techniques for conducting the research. The intention here is to attack this method not for any failure to accomplish what it sets out to do, but rather for its limits on what is explored. Thus, even with its considerable success in achieving its research goals its value in the study of politics and the legal process is limited.

LINGUISTIC ANALYSIS AND
JUDICIAL BEHAVIORALISM

A positivistic epistemology is the ground for most contemporary social scientific research. The dominance of this perspecitive is evident in the work of Karl Popper, Ernest Nagel, A. J. Ayer, Rudolf Carnap, Carl G. Hempel, and May Brodbeck.[2] These theorists of social science reflect the dichotomy between object and representation which is seen to exist in the empiricist theories of language (see Chapter 2). This dichotomy is the basis for the distinction between legitimate propositions which are either logically consistent or empirically verifiable. It is also the basis for the distinction between analytic and synthetic propositions which has produced other dichotomies that characterize investigation in the social sciences, such as between metaphysical and scientific realms, theory and observation, discovery and justification.[3]

Because the theoretical formulations of the enterprise govern how the process is carried on in natural as well as in social science, the conception of what it is possible to know and the process of investigation that such a conception entails reveal what is relevant to the description of political life. In addition, in the social sciences, the theoretical discussions of modes of investigation have been closely tied to defenses of particular traditions of research and inevitably to the validity and significance of their findings.[4] The theories have indicated the status not only of the various facets of political life under investigation, but also of the tools of explanation, such as the attitudes relied on so heavily by judicial behavioralists.[5] That a science of politics is to be modeled after the natural sciences is well known. The implications for the study of judicial decision, which in the form of judicial behavioralism is more derivative than any other area of investigation, is less fully comprehended.

Legal positivism thus distinguishes legal norms from the behavior of judges. For the most part, the norms fall into a metaphysical realm which is left to legal practitioners who may engage in manipulation of these symbols. In his *Pure Theory of Law*, Hans Kelsen makes an unusual contribution by attempting to assess norms on the basis of a model of logic.[6] For positivists operating in political science, the effort has been to construct models of explanation which are based in the empirical world of judicial action. A leading advocate of the behavioral methods examined here is Glendon Schubert. His observations on the place of his work and the critique of metaphysical jurisprudence is informative. He sees behavioralism as building systematic theory on the insight of legal realism.[7] His goal has been to develop empirical or scientific theory modeled after the natural sciences. The human qualities of judges are the key to the enterprise, and Schubert admits that the behavioral perspective has had little success in eroding the traditional mythology of mechanical jurisprudence in the eyes of "the judges themselves, practicing lawyers, journalists, and the public."[8]

According to positivism, what these practitioners, commentators, and observers believe is nonsense. A. J. Ayer states the position with regard to metaphysics in language as follows:

We may accordingly define a metaphysical sentence as a sentence which purports to express a genuine proposition, but does, in fact, express neither a tautology nor an empirical hypothesis. And as tautologies and empirical hypothesis form the entire class of significant propositions, we are justified in concluding that all metaphysical assertions are nonsensical.[9]

Legal assertions fall into this metaphysical realm. Because of their authoritative character, however, they are politically significant. Legal assertions, in an age of scientific explanation, have been held to be deficient in the one area in which they might at least be sensible—that of logic. But the premise of traditional jurisprudence, that judges rely on the use of logic, has not been tenable since the contributions of legal realism. Even metaphysics can be important if it has an authoritative base. In law, the base for decisions is the authority of the sovereign or the legitimacy of the system from which they are disseminated. Since legal assertions are not necessarily logical, it is the reality of judicial action in an authoritative sphere which is the foundation for political research.

Judicial behavioralism has contributed to a description of the political aspects of legal behavior through the "rule orientation" of traditional jurisprudence which has been its backdrop. The attention to what judges do, when employed as a measure of where a particular judge stands on an issue or in relation to an ideological position, has received widespread acceptance. We need go no further than the box scores that are now an annual feature of the *Harvard Law Review's* analysis of each Supreme Court term. However, the description of distinctly "legal" behavior as opposed to the behavior of judges per se is limited by traditional conceptions of law and scientific investigation. The dichotomy between law and behavior constrains inquiry into the "legal" aspects of what judges do.

Traditional empiricism is responsible for analysis of behavior that looks to rules in the form of precedent as the criteria for legal behavior. In this approach, legal precedents must have some observable impact on behavior in order to be considered significant as explanations of the judicial decision-making process. In most investigations of judicial behavior, the influence of law is measured by whether or not precedent is followed. Research of this nature, as conventionally operationalized, permits no intermediary position between "laws" on the one hand and "men" on the other. Inasmuch as it is fundamental to behavioral science, the dichotomy evident in this position has inhibited explanation of the legal process. It has driven a wedge between law, the nonfactual norms, and reality, the observable behavior of judges. The behavior of judges, although it tells "what the law is," is analytically distinguished from the body of "law."

Characterization of the limitations on understanding produced by the positivist dichotomy is not, however, to argue that there are not aspects of the legal process that can be properly placed on one side or the other of the distinction.[10] The first ten Amendments to the Constitution do define a galaxy of rights. It is false to say that Congress can act to limit freedom of speech where such an action is acknowledged to be a limitation in the constitutional sense, although it is often quite informative to investigate the extent to which the citizenry is free to say what it wishes. However, in the study of judicial decision, the extreme positions are not particularly enlightening. The enterprise is one of understanding action where it determines when traditional rights may be applicable to certain events. Neither the black letter law nor the practice of the body politic is the object of the investigation. Rather, it is the extent to which traditions that stand as rules to the citizen serve to inform and govern the choice of those who develop them.

When a linguistic model is applied to the explanation of legal behavior, the distinction becomes less rigid and a focus can be placed on the points where it breaks down. The measure of the extent to which behavior is "legal" need not be solely in terms of established law. It may be found in the use of legal language and the linguistic considerations that provide the background for interpretation. A linguistic theory of judicial decision attempts to present an alternative to the traditional distinction between rules and practice. This approach stands in relation to judicial behavioralism much as ordinary language philosophy stands in relation to the empiricist theories of language. In developing the ordinary language position, Wittgenstein believed that a proper conception of language would have to oscillate between "a kind of objectivism which tries to offer an independent support for linguistic practices," and a mere "description of the practices themselves."[11] He recognized that the description of the practices would have significance only against the backdrop of objectivism. Linguistic theory, by dealing with the substantive language of law as a factor in interpretive behavior, takes a middle ground between the two poles of positivism.

Interpretation is fundamental to even the ordinary use of language. It has been shown that the decision as to how to speak or write about a new situation is not a logical operation. Knowledge of a language cannot tell exactly how the language will be used in a new case. Thus, an element of creativity is entailed in using a language, but it is restrained creativity since it is based on linguistic competencies. In law, the judge makes conceptual judgments governed by linguistic factors. The way in which his training in the language of the law governs these judgments is the characteristic legal factor in judicial decision-making.

In one of the most widely read applications of ordinary language philosophy to the social sciences, Peter Winch employs Michael Oakeshott's metaphor to point out the limits of the positivist distinction between ideas and behavior: "A cook is not a man who first has a vision of a pie and then tries to make it; he is a man skilled in cookery, and both his projects and his acheivements spring from that skill."[12] Winch brings home the point as follows: "Generally, both the ends sought and the means employed in human life, so far from generating forms of social activity, depend for their very being on those forms."[13] The possession of certain competencies is what enables those who know a language to proceed both in ordinary discourse and in the special language of constitutional law. Both *what* we do and *how* we do it are dependent on the ways in which we have come to understand our activities. The use of legal language, like the use of ordinary language, entails some comprehension of the conventions associated with the particular linguistic vehicles used.[14]

In behavioral jurisprudence, the attitudinal or social background variables are extracted from a particular judicial decision so that the former are seen as independent variables and the latter as dependent. This position is useful in demonstrating what certain judges are likely to do. For students of judicial behavior who explicitly limit the application of their findings in this way, linguistic theory merely adds some depth to the explanation of the decision-making process. Quite often, however, the impact of behavioral science in this sphere is such that these social and attitudinal considerations stand in opposition to the law. In such cases, linguistic theory suggests a reconceptualization. Since the world is symbolized in language, the legal world is symbolized in its unique language. Robert Pranger, who owes much of his theory of symbolic action to Kenneth Burke, argues that "opinion is not only a 'response to,' but 'an act upon' a political world already symbolized in the actors' mind."[15] It is the language of constitutional law which symbolizes the world for the Supreme Court Justice considering claims brought in terms of the provisions of the Constitution. The contribution of linguistic theory to the explanation of judicial behavior is its consideration of law as having psycholinguistic significance. The examination of what is said, the use of words, is subject to empirical investigation. If the ways that a particular concept is used are examined and patterns are revealed for the concept, treatment of the concept as a grammatical criterion in the linguistic sense opens another area to investigation. The study of language takes for its data an entirely different sphere from that of behavioralism in law. Where behavioralism has been primarily concerned with the attitudinal differences among judges when they dissent on a case, the study of legal language explains the widespread similarities in judicial decision.

The present formulation of the nature of legal language has been drawn primarily from philosophy, but recent work relating the philosophical investigation of language to the study of the mind lays the foundation for the study of psycholinguistic factors in law.[16] Students of Wittgenstein have also related his work to Gestalt psychology.[17] Such applications suggest the possibility of examining the impact of the legal Gestalt on the psychological dimensions of judicial decision and of considering legal language as a mediating function in the judicial decision by its place in the judicial mind. However, the positivist theories in which behavioralism is rooted have constructed explanatory schemes which are built on factors dichotomized from the law. The significance of psycholinguistic insights for law must await further development of the theories themselves. It is for this reason that the characterization of judicial decision as rooted in constititional language suggests a dimension of the decision that must await further development.

THE BEHAVIORALIST
THEORY OF ATTITUDES

Judicial behavioralism builds its theory of explanation on a psychological model tied to a stimulus-response paradigm. C. Herman Pritchett first developed the empirical description of judicial decision from the study of voting blocs on the Supreme Court.[18] These blocs were distinguished by the Justices' positions on ideological continua which revealed judicial attitudes. Pritchett is said to have continued the realist tradition.[19] Indeed, his effort to focus on acts in order to help explain the rationales presented in opinions was an example of attention to the real rather than the metaphysical world. His demonstration of the political dimension of judicial action has been remarkably successful, and it has stimulated developments more self-consciously concerned with the goals of behavioral science. The blocs were used under the theory that similarity of attitude would be represented by unified voting patterns.[20] His major work in this area, the 1948 study of the Roosevelt Court, employed the attitude dimension to more fully explain the doctrinal contributions of this group of Justices.

The most dramatic development of the behavioral position was in the period from 1958[21] to 1965[22] with the "maturity" of the field in the work of Glendon Schubert. While he continues to be one of the most productive figures in contemporary political science, his major tenets and contributions were established during this period. Schubert refined the attitude dimension and the methods by which it was to be revealed, first through factor analysis and then through cumulative scaling. The fact situation stimulus was seen as mediated by attitude consideration which explained the behavioral response: "The questions of valuation raised by cases are the counterparts of the attitudes of the justices, which mediate the external values (represented by issues in cases) and the internal values (which constitute the beliefs of the individual justices)."[23] Thus, the "scientific" construct rather than the rationalizations provided in opinions explains judicial choice.[24] Schubert has continued to revise and develop the method, moving of late into spatial models, but the basic scheme remains the same.

The analytic background for this mode of investigation has seldom been more fully explained than in a recent work on Supreme Court decision-making by David W. Rohde and Harold J. Spaeth.[25] They describe beliefs, attitudes, and values as "constructs" which are the "artificial creation, of a scientist" and not "out there in the 'real' world."[26] Their formulation employs the attitude construct to explain the relation of personal policy preferences to the judicial decision. They adapt an established definition of attitudes.

An attitude is a (1) relatively enduring, (2) organization of interrelated beliefs that describe, evaluate, and advocate action with respect to an object or situation, (3) with each belief having cognitive, affective, and behavioral components. (4) Each one of these beliefs is a predisposition that, when suitably activated, results in some preferential response for that attitude object or situation, or toward the maintenance or preservation of the attitude itself.[27]

An important limitation on this theory is the relationship it postulates between what it chooses to investigate and the legal form by which it is commonly identified. Not words but deeds, actions, and votes are the key to the judicial mind. In a discussion on which Glendon Schubert[28] relies, Reed Lawlor proposed that *"stare decisis* is to be expressed in terms of facts, not in terms of judicial reasoning or legal principles.''[29] A similarity with positivism in the study of language is obvious; and the capacity of the behavioral model to explain the judicial decision is thereby limited. In Lawlor's formulation, the significance of legal constructs is beyond the scope of the investigation. In a comprehensive effort to show how judges function as policy-makers, the symbolic field is at least as important as judicial attitudes. *Stare decisis* may well be left as a psychological variable, but the substance of prior opinions, to the extent that they reveal the terrain of the law, must be incorporated in a central position in a theory of judicial decision.

T. L. Becker has been critical of the behavioral operationalization of judicial attitude. It seems to him to be circular since Schubert and others use the response itself, the facts as contained in the opinion, as the stimulus.[30] Rohde and Spaeth recognize that the attitude scales depend on the "legal and semantic categories into which the Court's decision making may be divided.''[31] They argue, however, that "neither the fact that the categories are initially established by means of an intuitive content analysis . . . nor the fact that the resulting category scales are less than ideally refined, gainsays the validity of the theory.''[32] Validity is to be a function of explanatory and predictive power. In this formulation, the emphasis on prediction turns attention from the problem of circularity. But in order to explain what is going on, any theory of a judicial decision would have to explain the nature of the choices available to the Justices, and not just a stand on one side or the other with regard to the outcome of a case. In any event, the existence of personal considerations influencing the vote on cases before the Supreme Court has been adequately demonstrated. What has not yet been explained is the role of law in the decision.

It is in this regard that linguistic theory allows the exercise of judicial discretion to be viewed in terms of the grammar of legal language. The function of legal language is akin to the mediation processes which alter the rigid stimulus-response paradigm. But since they are characteristic of the stimuli themselves they cannot stand in the same explanatory scheme as attitudes. The result has been a tendency to ignore the impact of law in the judicial decision.

Schubert made such an error in his analysis of the Warren Court when he failed to consider *stare decisis* as a behavioral constraint on the decision-making of judges.[33] The oversight seems to have resulted from his predisposition to show the nonlegal or personal dimensions of the judicial decision: "The question to which I address myself is this: When men play political roles, to what extent are their public acts influenced by their personal beliefs?"[34] The personal considerations which Schubert looks for are attitudinal. A result of the dichotomy between law and behavior is that attitudes have often been explored as if they were devoid of legal considerations. In fact, attitudes are only evident with reference to language, and legal attitudes are dependent on legal language.

In the same year that Schubert's own research brought out his failure to consider *stare decisis* in his explanatory design of the judicial decision, he wrote that judicial behavior studies had substantially "debunked legal principles as factors controlling decision."[35] This paradox is cited by Becker in support of his argument that any recognition of *stare decisis* as a factor in the judicial decision demonstrates that there is a role expectation that legal doctrine must control decisions.[36] From a linguistic point of view, the function of principles in the judicial process is something other than the type of control mechanism attacked by Schubert and sought by Becker. In the case of Schubert, rather than debunking legal principles, he has simply chosen not to examine them. Given the degree to which Becker's formulation depends on the traditional conception of *stare decisis,* his investigation of the unique legal considerations which separate the judge from other political actors is also conceptually limited.[37]

The idea that the decisions of judges are "political" when personal opinion plays a role and "legal" when precedent governs an opinion is based on an identification of "law" with precedent. Since discretion is a recognized element of decisions in language, the linguistic theory of judicial decision-making suggests that such behavioral constructs as attitude have a bearing on the judicial decision along with, rather than in opposition to, legal considerations evident in the language of law.

Significant depth is added to the description of dissent behavior by Ulmer and others in their correlation of dissent with social background factors. Ulmer views a judicial decision as "a response to certain stimuli after they have been filtered through a set of system properties."[38] Ulmer considers both organic (physical) and psychological characteristics of the decision-maker in the systemic properties, and he breaks down stimuli into (a) those primarily flowing from the cases being litigated and (b) contextual-environmental factors.[39] In the tradition of this method of analysis, the characteristics are not legal. Ulmer examines the situation of a black litigant that suggests one response to judges, while potential charges of racism may arise as a countervailing contextual factor.

A similar model is the basis for Joseph Tanenhaus's discussion of cues influencing the determination of *certiorari* jurisdiction.[40] Tanenhaus was able to explain 25 to 43 percent of the cases in which *certiorari* was granted by means of political cues such as (a) whether the government was a party, (b) whether there had been dissension in appellate opinions on the case, and (c) whether the issue concerned civil liberties or economics. It should be made clear, although it seldom is, that because of the dichotomy between law and behavior, such characterizations still exclude legal considerations.

In a theoretically more elaborate enterprise, Rohde and Spaeth also exclude legal dimensions from their theory of explanation. They emphasize the range of precedent, generally failing to note the limits of that range, except in "the most commonplace cases."[41] A seemingly unlimited range of discretion is seen as characteristic of the political realm in which attitudes operate. The ability of the Supreme Court Justice to justify almost any decision is the byword. The range of this implicit but seldom acknowledged limit is the domain revealed by the grammar of constitutional language.

LAW IN JUDICIAL DECISION

The shift from the study of what judges have said to what makes judges behave as they do is attributed to C. Herman Pritchett.[42] This shift is the foundation for the present suggestion that *behavior* in a linguistic context can be partly explained by reference to what has been said. Language bridges the formerly polar positions of law and behavior and presents a new method for analyzing what makes judges behave as they do.

Judicial behavioralism's contribution, like that of legal realism, depends on a contrast with traditional jurisprudence. But the contrast inhibits its capacity to explain what is unique in judicial activity. Behavioralism has presumed precedent orientation to be a criterion for *legal* behavior. It holds deference to precedent to be a requirement for the determination that legal factors constrain the judges.[43] However, the focus of behavioralism has been elsewhere. Thus, the description of distinctly "legal" aspects of judicial behavior is limited by the very perspective which is behavioralism's *raison d'etre*. This type of research, as conventionally operationalized, is governed by a more complicated version of the popular distinction between "laws" and "men." The distinction fails to represent the deeper significance which the legal tradition has for judicial decision.

The relation of language to action is not a predictive one. Action in the legal system is intentional. It is purposeful action. In attempting to chart the bounds of legal action, especially as it might be evident in appellate judiciaries, there is little one can do about the judge who acts under duress or inattention and whose cognitive capacities are not engaged in the process of deciding. Where legal categories comprise the body of discourse, however, students of judicial decision must be attentive to the conceptual capacities and the necessary linguistic competencies that function as prerequisites to action. Where opinions are the evidence of conceptual structures there is a leap of faith that the judges are "involved." It is a faith as central to behavioralism as to a model of decision based on language. At least initially, it seems necessary. Subsequently, use of constitutional language in situations like oral argument, even before a decision has been reached, may be a more appropriate source of the data necessary to show the conceptual baggage the Justices take into the conference room.

While behavioralists assert that the verbal substance of the opinion has no necessary connection with the decisional outcome, a sensitivity to linguistic constructs shows that the sense of the law which is acquired from opinions is a prerequisite for considering any particular case. Although behavioralists may concede that conventional legal usage determines the form an opinion will take, they deny that these conventions can explain a particular outcome. Their position is only partly accurate given the role of language in presenting the world. There is compelling evidence that in judicial interpretation, particular case situations are filtered through legal language. It is, therefore, important to distinguish the decision in a particular case (the focus of behavioralists) from the conceptual boundaries of the legal tradition that reveal the limits of sensibility in appellate adjudication.

In the model suggested by Schubert, "the cases on the Court's dockets are conceptualized as complex stimuli, which (in effect) ask questions about issues to which the justices are asked to respond."[44] In the linguistic model, the response to an issue presented by a case would be governed by the grammatical considerations relevant to that issue. The conceptualization of the decision could be formulated in terms of "generative grammars" which would describe the process of making a legal statement in a novel context.[45] The construction and interpretation of sentences in language, which enables the native speaker to build a potentially infinite number of intelligible sentences,[46] is a process which has been suggested to be akin to interpretation in law. It may be that the techniques by which sentences are broken down by linguists to demonstrate the "deep structures" underlying the use of language can be applied to law.

The fact that grammatical considerations govern appellate judicial decisions need not detract from analysis of personal preferences. Rather, the linguistic aspects of constitutional law add another dimension to the description of judicial interpretation which may partially explain such factors as the degree to which dissent remains exceptional at the appellate level. In the past, behavioralism has looked to institutional pressures and personal interpretations of the restraints on a particular role to explain "the push toward consensus."[47] The linguistic aspects of law explain the operation of a similar "push toward consensus" in language which is a product of the grammatical considerations that enable certain operations to be performed. Activity in accordance with convention is explained by the development of linguistic capacities rather than by rules as restraints on behavior.

Because consideration of the linguistic aspects of legal behavior alters the epistemological view of legal interpretation, the traditional description of the exercise of discretion must be reexamined. By describing discretion as characteristic of the use of concepts in legal language, it is no longer appropriate to suggest that there is law "over here" and a decision "over there."[48] There may indeed be a particular rule "here" and a decision which seems to come from "over there," but the impact of the grammar of legal language on judicial behavior is missed if the criteria for a "legal" decision are tied to prior rules in the form of precedent. This redefinition gives depth to the principle of *stare decisis*. It demands a change in the traditional interpretation of judicial decision. The enduring power of the law, traditionally defined in terms of *stare decisis* or precedent orientation, is an orientation of the Justice, the decision to adhere to a norm. As the conceptual basis for a decision in a legal case, law may more profitably be seen as determining what is appropriate at a level beneath the issues in controversy in a case but nevertheless determining the entire conceptual arrangement that enables a case to be brought and decided.

Martin Shapiro, a "traditionalist" with an interest in communication theory, has described why even a dominant judicial attitude will not necessarily result in a court's overall impact being absolutely consistent with that attitude. The situation is a result of the doctrinal parameters.[49] For Shapiro, the crucial concept is plausibility. It is only plausible claims that a particular judge will have occasion to decide. Plausibility is a function of the state of the doctrine, and it is thus "a matter of the verbal propositions of the law . . . rather than the attitudinal pattern of the judge in individual cases."[50] He emphasizes decisions because it is communication through the announced holding that is the key to plausibility. Language analysis complements Shapiro's theory by focusing on meaning and the interrelations between concepts on which plausibility or the "sense" of a claim is conveyed.

A recent effort to integrate public law and judicial behavior by Victor Flango and Craig Ducat[51] reveals continued awareness of the unsatisfactory state of scholarship on the judicial decision. Relying on nonunanimous cases, like the earlier work, the authors propose an approach to the behavioral study of appellate judges relying on justification of the decision rather than inferences about judicial attitudes. They are sensitive to the conceptual dimension to the extent that they rely on opinions to reveal the judge's view of the law. Although the model goes beyond the traditional behavioral dependence on attitudes, it substitutes other constructs based on a hypothesis about how judges approach their world. The model relies on the judicial role which it takes as characterized by "the judge's approach to law, and his conception of the relationship between the judiciary and the other branches of government."[52] The approach comes down to being a methodologically complex assessment of judicial role, and it may form a link, in public law scholarship, between role theory and behavioral studies of attitudes. In this regard, much that is said about judicial role in Chapter 5 is applicable to the Flango and Ducat model.

Analysis of the judicial decision from the perspective of language links communication in the law with investigations into other symbolic processes, thereby suggesting a variety of approaches to the nature of legal learning and conceptual change. Rather than detracting from the significance of personal preferences, my perspective on constitutional law develops other relevant characteristics of the decision. These characteristics are politically significant because they determine what the Justices will be asked to consider as well as the language of their response. The grammatical revelations serve as a source for delineating a legal structure that transcends both the surface level of doctrinal debate and the outcomes with which it is associated. The linguistic aspects of the legal tradition explain the operation of legal compulsion due to the experience that enables legal professionals to communicate. Activity in accordance with convention is explained by the development of linguistic capacities, knowledge of sense and structure, rather than by rules.

Students of politics will no doubt remain interested in identifying liberal and conservative judges, since it has become widely accepted that "the exercise of judicial discretion is, in a real sense, political decision-making."[53] But "discretion," when exercised within a conceptual tradition, may be characterized as "legal" if the effective cognitive limits on choice are products of that tradition. This broadened view of the legal part of judicial decision suggests that attitudinal considerations operate along with, rather than in opposition to, the meaning and structure evident in constitutional language.

NOTES

1. Glendon Schubert, *Human Jurisprudence: Public Law as Political Science* (Honolulu: University Press of Hawaii, 1975); *The Judicial Mind Revisited* (New York: Oxford University Press, 1974); "The Rhetoric of Constitutional Change," *Journal of Public Law* 16: 16-50; "A Psychological Model of Supreme Court Decision-Making," and "Prediction from a Psychometric Model," *Judicial Behavior,* ed. Glendon Schubert (Chicago: Rand McNally and Co., 1964), p. 1; *The Judicial Mind: The Attitudes and Ideologies of Supreme Court Justices, 1946-1963* (Evanston, Ill.: Northwestern University Press, 1965); *Quantitative Analysis of Judicial Behavior* (New York: Free Press, 1959). S. S. Ulmer, "Dissent Behavior and the Social Background of Supreme Court Justices," *Journal of Politics* 32 (1970):580; "The Discriminant Function and a Theoretical Context for Its Use in Estimating the Votes of Judges," *The Frontiers of Judicial Research*, eds. Joel Grossman and Joseph Tanenhaus (New York: John Wiley and Sons, 1969), pp. 335-369. David W. Rohde and Harold J. Spaeth, *Supreme Court Decision Making* (San Francisco: W. H. Freeman and Co., 1976).

2. Gunnell, op. cit.

3. Ibid., pp. 9-10.

4. Robert Dahl, "The Behavioral Approach in Political Science: Epitaph for a Monument to a Successful Protest," in *Behavioralism in Political Science,* ed. Heinz Eulau (New York: Atherton Press, 1969); David Easton, "The New Revolution in Political Science," *American Political Science Review* 63 (1969):1501-1061; Heinz Eulau, *The Behavioral Persuasion in Politics* (New York: Random House, 1963).

5. Gunnell, op. cit., Chapter 1.

6. Hans Kelsen, *Pure Theory of Law* (Berkeley: University of California Press, 1967).

7. Schubert, *Human Jurisprudence,* p. 43.

8. Ibid.

9. A. J. Ayer, *Language, Truth and Logic* (New York: Dover, 1946), p. 40.

10. See Connolly, op. cit., pp. 17-22.

11. David Pears, *Ludwig Wittgenstein* (New York: Viking Press, 1969), p. 182.

12. Winch, op. cit., pp. 54-55.

13. Ibid., p. 55.

14. See Adam Schaff, *Language and Cognition* (New York: McGraw-Hill, 1973), p. 82.

15. Robert Pranger, *Action, Symbolism and Order* (Nashville, Tenn.: Vanderbilt University Press, 1968), p. 190.

16. Jerry Fodor and Jerrold Katz, op. cit.; Noam Chomsky, *Language and Mind* (New York: Harcourt, Brace and Co., 1968); Harrison, op. cit.

17. W.W. Bartley, *Wittgenstein* (Philadelphia: Lippincott, 1973); Allan Janik and Stephen Toulmin, *Wittgenstein's Vienna* (New York: Simon and Schuster, 1973).

18. Pritchett, "Divisions of Opinion Among Justices of the United States Supreme Court, 1939-41," *American Political Science Review* 35 (1941): 890-898; *The Roosevelt Court.*

19. Sheldon Goldman, *The Federal Courts as a Political System,* 2nd ed. (New York: Harper and Row, 1976).

20. Ibid., p. 161.

21. Schubert, "The Study of Judicial Decision-Making as an Aspect of Political Behavior," *American Political Science Review* 52 (1958): 1007-1025.

22. Schubert, *The Judicial Mind.*

23. Goldman, op. cit., p. 160.

24. Schubert, *Judicial Mind*, p. 38.

25. Rohde and Spaeth, op. cit.

26. Ibid., p. 75.

27. Ibid., adapted from Milton Rokeach, "The Nature of Attitudes," in *International Encyclopedia of the Social Sciences*, 1968 ed., Vol. 1, pp. 449-457.

28. Schubert, *Judicial Mind Revisited,* p. 20; see Reed C. Lawlor, "Personal Stare Decisis," *Southern California Law Review* 41 (1967): 73-118.

29. Schubert, "Rhetoric," p. 81.

30. Theodore L. Becker, *Political Behavioralism and Modern Jurisprudence* (Chicago: Rand McNally, 1964), p. 14.

31. Rohde and Spaeth, op. cit., p. 87.

32. Ibid.

33. Glendon Schubert, "Civilian Control and Stare Decisis in the Warren Court," *Judicial Decision-Making*, ed. Glendon Schubert (New York: Free Press, Macmillan, 1953), p. 73.

34. Schubert, *Judicial Mind,* p. 15.

35. G. Schubert, "Judicial Attitudes and Voting Behavior," *Law and Contemporary Problems* 28 (Winter 1963): 104.

36. T. L. Becker, *Comparative Judicial Politics* (Chicago: Rand McNally and Co., 1970), pp. 28-29.

37. See Chapter 5.

38. Ulmer, op. cit., p. 583.

39. Ibid.

40. Joseph Tanenhaus, et al., "The Supreme Court's Certiorari Jurisdiction: Cue Theory," in Schubert, op. cit.

41. Rohde and Spaeth, op. cit., p. 35.

42. Grossman and Tannenhaus, eds., op. cit.

43. Schubert, *Judicial Mind.*

44. Ibid., p. 37.

45. Noam Chomsky, *Current Issues in Linguistic Theory* (The Hague: Monton and Co., 1964).

46. For the discussion of the process in language, see Bernard Harrison, *Form and Content* (Oxford: Basil Blackwell, 1973), especially pp. 13-14.

47. Joel B. Grossman, "Social Backgrounds and Judicial Decisions: Notes for a Theory," *Journal of Politics* 29 (1967): 342.

48. Probert, *Law, Language and Communication,* p. 6.

49. Martin Shapiro, *The Supreme Court and Administrative Agencies* (New York: Free Press, 1968), pp. 39-43.

50. Ibid., p. 43.

51. Victor E. Flango and Craig R. Ducat, "Toward an Integration of Public Law and Judicial Behavior," *The Journal of Politics* 39 (1977): 41-72.

52. Ibid., p. 48.

53. Sheldon Goldman, "Conflict on the U.S. Courts of Appeals 1965-1971: A Quantitative Analysis," *University of Cincinnati Law Review* 42 (1973): 655-658.

4 | Structure and Language in the Constitution

Two levels of investigation are appropriate to the study of constitutional language. The first, which is the subject of this chapter, explores the relevance of linguistic theories to the meaning evident in the document. The investigation is undertaken to establish the linguistic dimensions of the document, and not to describe the substance of adjudication. Modern linguistic theory also suggests that the tradition of interpretation that constitutes constitutional law may be described as a language. This notion is to be demonstrated by revealing the degree to which unique practices exist that determine what the Justices can say about the Constitution. A full elaboration of these practices follows an exploration of some similarities between ordinary language and Supreme Court decisions about the Constitution. These factors are shown to be the sort of qualities that comprise a unique language. Understanding of these factors is facilitated by the present investigation of the relation between meaning and the use of language evident in the document.

The meaning of the document is not self-evident, but can be shown through analysis of its language. The investigation here suggests the range of meanings and the way they are carried by the structural relations in the text. The emphasis of the present discussion is on the way the members of the Constitutional Convention presented their scheme. This perspective presumes neither that the words in the document are the only basis for interpretation nor that they have served as rules for judicial decision. They are presented here as a foundation so obvious that it is often altogether overlooked. This investigation examines the document on the basis of which constitutional law has been developed. The very fact that the interpretive tradition has developed with reference to the document establishes its relevance for revealing the structure of judicial decision. In the investigation, consideration is given to the differences in meaning that become evident as a result of (1) different classes of words being joined together, (2) different syntactical contexts, and (3) different requirements for substitution of appropriate words.

LANGUAGE AND CONCEPTUAL STRUCTURES

The meanings associated with human expression depend on convention. Whether it be "a cuneiform inscription of the words the Tigris boatman shouts"[1] or the invocation of the due process clause of the Constitution to enable a woman to have an abortion, conventions characterize the utterances. In the study of language, this body of experience is called "grammar." Problems with the traditional notion of grammar have, in the last two decades, received the attention of students of both linguistics and the philosophy of language. This attention has led to some significant alterations of how we understand the nature of these conventions. These disciplines share a recognition that the nature of grammar is neither determined nor explained by the prescriptive rules that have traditionally been associated with its study. The present examination is derived from Wittgenstein and students who have adopted his insights into the nature of language. Their work should be distinguished from a discussion of grammar in terms of prescriptive rules for the correct use of language. The elements of "grammar" which bear on the Constitution are not limited to the "subject-predicate-object" type, although the syntactic structure of sentences is one approach to meaning in language which is considered here. Ordinary language philosophy moves from the description and analysis of proper speech to recording how language is used and the limits of intelligibility.

The source of such an investigation in ordinary language is the use of the language by those for whom it is a means of communication. As Stanley Cavell points out in discussing the nature of the philosophical investigation of language, it is proper for the native speaker to rely on his knowledge of the language.[2] Of course, an individual can be mistaken in specifying the criteria for the appropriate use of a word, but a mistake is an unusual, often unintelligible use. These mistakes can also offer important insights into the subtleties of our use of language.[3] The way language is used constitutes data for investigating the meaning relied on in human communication because "a natural language is what native speakers of that language speak."[4]

The present study does not attempt to formalize the grammatical properties evident in the Constitution. The discussion of these properties will show that, although it is a legal document, much about the Constitution can be studied in the same fashion as ordinary language. It is in this sense that the linguistic capacities of a native speaker of English are a guide to the judicial decision. The analysis of ordinary language attempts to demonstrate the conventions that govern the ways words can be put together. In a like manner, the language in the Constitution can be investigated by relying on knowledge of the way language is used. Thus, the investigation of constitutional language establishes a perspective.

The philosophical investigation of language examines how it is used rather than why it is used in a particular way. This approach is taken because it is believed that language use has an autonomy that belies explanation: "Philosophy may in no way interfere with the actual use of language; it can in the end only describe it. For it can not give any foundations either. It leaves everything as it is."[5] The philosophical investigation of ordinary language leaves everything the way it is, asserting that "reasons" or grounds that stand as *more* certain than beliefs themselves do not exist. Hence, philosophy in this sense does not supply us with any justification for our beliefs, although it may succeed in pointing out some of the causes for belief.[6] In this sense, the student of language in the Constitution is an observer rather than a participant. However, it is in the nature of this activity that the careful observation of language in the Constitution allows for a fuller description of its influence on judicial decision.

The bedrock of philosophical investigation is the fact that we use language in certain ways. The search for meaning in language leads to an investigation of language use. Such an investigation considers the activities and practices which determine and give rise to linguistic meaning. "It is what human beings say that is true or false; and they agree in the language they use."[7] The way language is used tells us something about the nature of the activities in which we engage; the study of language tells us how we understand or make sense of the world.

Given the focus on language, a grammatical investigation, by describing the ways in which we use words, seeks to reveal the nature of the subjects under investigation. The desire to explain, in any "justificatory" sense, why we use language in the ways we do must of necessity be resisted. To ask for explanation or justification at this level is similar to asking, as Wittgenstein often points out, whether we are justified in being human beings. Such questions "seem to drag everything with (them) and plunge (them) into chaos."[8]

The "grammar" of the human activities which are the focus of the investigation of language tells us specifically what these activities are, i.e., how they fit into the entire web of human behavior. We learn what the activities are by learning how they fit. Hence, knowing the "grammar" of a language is the necessary basis from which we acquire the meaning of words.

Hubert Schwyzer points out why it is important to concentrate on language use and on what it reveals.[9] Language is the source of our understanding of the activities in which we engage. For example, we cannot have a desire or intention to convey the fact that we "feel pain" to another person apart from a linguistic activity such as "complaining of pain." Modern linguistic theory eliminates the distinction in the empiricist position between so-called real pain and the expression of pain.

There may, of course, be "pain" without the "expression of pain," but we can only understand it if we already know what it is to "be in pain" or "complain of pain." Schwyzer elaborates this position in arguing that "knowing what it is to complain of pain" is a prerequisite to knowing "what it is to intend to convey the fact that one feels pain." We cannot even know what pain is without knowing what it is to complain of or express pain. These linguistic activities give the meaning of "pain" to us.

According to philosophical investigations of ordinary language,

there is no real pain which our expressions merely try to approximate. Language tells us what pain really is. The limitations of the
view that language is only a "symbol" or "picture" of reality were
considered in the previous chapter. The present discussion of the
grammar in the Constitution elaborates the ways in which language
is itself the source of meaning upon which we necessarily rely.
Language tells what kind of things are contained in the Constitution. The grammar of the language in the Constitution reveals what
it makes sense to say about these things. Because language is itself
meaningful, the use of language in constitutional law is an
important factor in judicial interpretation. The epistemological
position of ordinary language philosophy introduced in the second
chapter entails that the traditional distinction seen to exist between
language and reality be eliminated. Such a distinction has circum-
scribed the description of judicial interpretation. The desire to find
the "real law" that underlies ordinary judicial decision is superseded if one accepts that judicial interpretation may be considered a
linguistic activity. Accordingly, the investigation of legal language
tells us what kind of things legal words and relations are and, in
turn, what "law" amounts to.

According to the philosophy of language, one might view the
words of the Constitution, like the words of ordinary language, as
meaningful not because they refer to specific elements of the world
but because their use is governed by conventions akin to
grammar.[10] It is not prescriptive rules which determine the relationship between the word and the thing signified, but it is the place the
word occupies in the grammatical structure of language which gives
meaning to words.[11] The goal here is to show the ways in which
words occupy places in these grammatical or linguistic structures.
Since the focus is on constitutional law, the function of grammar is
shown by examining the way in which linguistic considerations
reveal the meaning of the Constitution.

One of the insights accorded to Wittgenstein is his criticism of a
prevalent conception of language which proposes that we ought to
proceed in language according to strict rules. The rules are often
taken to represent the correct or ideal language. Ideal languages,
like logic, are seen by some as a goal. Wittgenstein cautions against
the mistake of viewing the ideal formulations as something which

we can approximate when we use language.[12] It is also necessary to avoid ideal formulations if we are to transcend the positivist trap in portraying judicial decision.

The contribution of ordinary language philosophy is the recognition that it is misleading to consider the ordinary use of language as somehow imperfect since use rather than the "ideal" rules is the basis of communication. It is because the conventional is important that philosophers of ordinary language have avoided rigorous formulation of rules of grammar. Their approach has been to discover the ways in which conventions influence language use. This approach has broken down the distinction between normative propositions and actual facts. Conventions, not prescriptive rules, show the meaning.

For Wittgenstein, the meaning of the elements in language and the use we make of language are described in terms of what he calls "language games." Toulmin describes these "games" as symbolic activities within which language and its elements are generally used.[13] The significance of conventions in language is a result of the "patterns of activities," e.g., "forms of life" out of which they arise.

It is consistent with the insight of ordinary language philosophy that an activity such as law creates a unique sphere in which a variety of meaningful activities are carried on. We understand these activities, i.e., we have some idea of what constitutes the legal "form of life," when we become familiar with the conventions that comprise the activity of interpreting the Constitution. The grammatical structures evident in the Constitution indicate the kinds of interpretations that are possible with regard to the words and concepts in the Constitution. The analysis of meaning consists of "giving the rules for the use of a particular sign."[14] "Rules" of this sort emerge from the analysis of use. They are not rules which show what it is appropriate to do, but rather a method for describing how language operates: ". . . grammar includes all the enormous number of conventions which, though nowhere expressly formulated, are presupposed in the understanding of everyday language."[15] Descriptive rules are derived from the conventions in terms of which we make sense in language. They follow from, rather than determine, linguistic meaning.

The appropriateness of looking at judicial interpretation from a linguistic perspective depends to a great extent on the insight of ordinary language philosophy which proposes that language consists of actions that may be characterized as decisions to proceed in one way rather than another. According to Waismann, these decisions are the result of a half-conscious pull.[16] We are drawn by experience to perform in a certain way. Language is based on experience, and the impact of this experience on the decision to proceed has also been described in terms of "signposts."[17]

There is room for doubt in the decision as to the appropriateness of utterances, since nothing in our use of language ultimately compels a particular response. However, the fact of doubt sometimes occurring and sometimes not is outside the realm of philosophy. Philosophical investigations merely show the kinds of signposts that exist. Such investigations cannot determine how the signposts will be taken by the user of language. Nor is it the philosopher's province to list each instance. These are empirical questions.[18]

Because ordinary language philosophy is to some extent a reaction against the notion that philosophers should be involved in seeking right action on the basis of normative rules, the philosophical investigations describe actions. This is a reflection of the fact in language that justification must cease at some point and that the individual, especialy if he is a judge, must proceed. "Explanation serves to remove or to avert a misunderstanding—one, that is, that would occur but for the explanation; not every one that I can imagine."[19] This point suggests the limits of an orientation that occurs in the study of interpretation in constitutional law. The style of Supreme Court opinions encourages us to see the reasons given for a decision as the grounds on which the decision is made. But in the law, as in language, justification cannot explain human action in the scientific sense. There are always other possible explanations, some of which bear on the substance of the controversy and others which do not. Explanations in law serve more than to remove misunderstandings; indeed, they are the stuff of the tradition of constitutional interpretation. Of course, we might say that any number of decisions are possible in a case before the Supreme Court, but the possibility of grounding a choice in an intelligible explanation limits the range of discussion. Only a finite number of concepts can be brought to bear, and they can only be used in a finite number of ways. By describing the constraints on the Justices in terms of the symbols available in the constitutional tradition, the student of the decision can focus on the intelligible options open to a Justice. The conventions in the Constitution, as in language, reveal the possibilities that are available if a Justice wishes to make sense. It is primarily to indicate the range of choices and the nature of the limits on that range, rather than to indicate why a particular choice is made, that ordinary linguistic competencies are relevant to judicial decision. This is not, of course, the traditional enterprise of students of constitutional law. It has been undertaken because traditional approaches, by focusing on the prediction and explanation of choice, have been unable to characterize the judicial decision as constraining action in any meaningful way.

We can describe linguistic conventions and develop some sense of how they operate; yet, we cannot ultimately determine how they will affect the behavior of a particular speaker. We cannot, for instance, determine which kind of rules will be taken to be essential and which inessential. In the exploration of the differences in meaning, the question arises as to what matters in determining those differences. In Waismann's words, it is a "decision to judge that the usage in the two cases is different."[20] Employing one of the clues to differences in meaning, Waismann argues that the question of whether words are interchangeable is ultimately a matter of choice. Where we find that the same word does not make sense in two contexts, we might still wish to say that these contexts are not significantly different. Waismann discusses the use of "make" in the phrases "to make a boat" and "to make a key." In the first case, "build" might be used for "make"; in the second, "cut" is more appropriate. Yet, he concludes, "the meaning is the same in both cases, for although the substitution rules are different, this difference is not relevant."[21] That is, most competent speakers of the language would not consider it relevant. Since linguistic conventions may be considered "sign-posts," they necessarily involve an interpretive function in their manner of operating. There are both essential and inessential conventions for determin-

ing how someone will respond when asked what he understands by
"ship." If by way of an answer he points to a ship, he might be
asked further if it is essential that we refer to a ship as "she" rather
than "it." If he says "no," he acknowledges the convention which
declares that in this case the gender of the word is not essential.

Much more is at stake in constitutional law than in language in
determining essential and inessential conventions, but that does not
provide a basis for claiming that the symbolic processes operate any
differently. Judges who make this determination from their own
experience, which is necessarily a mix of the professional and the
personal, must rely on the traditions of what they understand to be
appropriate. In a classic constitutional example, twenty years ago
the Justices of the Supreme Court began to determine what legal
requirements were "the very essence of a scheme of ordered
liberty."[22] Although the conventions relied on were for the most
part products of the legal tradition,[23] they were unknown to most
American citizens. The determination of the essential and inessential was a matter of choice among *those* alternatives. In *Palko v.
Connecticut* (1937),[24] Cardozo found that a particular retrial did
not constitute a violation of the double jeopardy provisions to such
an extent that it would be within that "essence," and ten years later
Justice Reed found that a requirement of testimony was not
implicit in the concept.[25] Others disagreed both as to what kind of
things were essential and, of course, as to whether the concept was
relevant at all.[26]

INVESTIGATING THE STRUCTURE OF
CONSTITUTIONAL LANGUAGE

The language of the Constitution depends on the language of
related activities to such an extent that interpretation in constitutional law is influenced by the established linguistic conventions of
those activities. Although the word "Senator" is defined in the
Constitution, the relationship between the Senate and the Congress
depends on the language of the statements in which they are defined. That "Congress . . . shall consist of a Senate and a House of
Representatives" is a statement which relies for its meaning not on
individual words but on the relations established between the

bodies by the predicate "shall consist of." The meaning of "Senate" and "House" is a function of their relation to each other and to the meaning of "Congress." The tradition from which the Constitution has developed establishes the conventions which constitute its grammar.

In *The Principles of Linguistic Philosophy*, Waismann describes three situations in language that result in different meanings. The situations he outlines are used in the remainder of this chapter to explore the force of grammar in the language of the Constitution. According to Waismann, a word may be treated as having different meanings if "it is used in different ways," i.e., (a) joined to words belonging to different word classes ("5 consists of 2 and 3," "water consists of oxygen and hydrogen"), (b) used in different syntactical contexts, or (c) used according to different substitution rules ("The rose is red," "Two times two is four").[27] While these instances do not give all the possible sources of difference in meaning, they do provide a method of demonstrating the ways in which meaning is revealed in language. Since the aim here is merely to suggest the utility of investigation into the language of law, the methods suggested by Waismann serve as an introduction. They provide the groundwork for discussing the significance of linguistic considerations of constitutional interpretation.

(A) JOINING DIFFERENT "WORD CLASSES"

Different classes or categories of words influence the meaning of the words which join them. This thesis can be demonstrated by an investigation into how these categories and classes give rise to the complexities in constitutional language. The meaning of the word "shall," which appears throughout the Constitution, is closely tied to the context in which it appears because of its auxiliary capacity. In the following examples, "shall" joins different classes of words. In each case, because of the nature of the words it joins, "shall" has a different meaning.

(1) The Vice-President of the United States *shall* be President of the Senate, . . .

(2) Each House *shall* be the Judge of the Elections, Returns and Qualifications . . .

(3) All legislative Powers herein granted *shall* be vested in a Congress of the United States, . . .

(4) The actual Enumeration *shall* be made within three years . . . [Italics mine]

In example (1), an office, the Vice-Presidency, is united with another position that the holder of the office is directed to assume. The character of the office of Vice-President has been indicated by its relation to that of the Presidency. The nature of the new position, President of the Senate, has not been specified, but it is evident from what is already known about the offices. "Vice-President" is in the same class of words as "President." Both suggest individual persons holding positions of authority. In crucial respects, however, they differ from "House" in example (2), which, among other things, suggests a deliberative body. Since presiding officers have a special relationship to legislative bodies, what they "shall be" is governed by this relationship. One could imagine a situation in which a presiding officer was not a single person, perhaps a triumvirate. In such a case, it would not be inconceivable to imagine an assembly. But the activity of presiding as revealed in the discussion of the functions of the President of the Senate and as it exists in ordinary English is difficult to correlate with assemblies. The categories of things that "shall" are related to reveal its meaning for those who know the language.

When joining one office, the Vice-Presidency, with another position, that of President of the Senate, in example (1), the directive "shall be" differs in meaning from example (2) where it joins a legislative body, the House, with its capacity to judge its members' qualifications. It is a different kind of activity for the Vice-President to be the President of the Senate than for the House to be the Judge of the Elections, and so forth. In the first case, a person is to assume a role or responsibility. It is an activity of involvement, or identity, like being a quarterback. In example (2), new powers of a legislative body are delineated. This is an extension more in the manner of what is already known or has already been designated with regard to the Houses. The phrase specifies not a whole new role, but a capacity within an established role, like the quarterack "being" the signal caller.

In cases (3) and (4), the different sorts of things "legislative Powers" are as compared to "Enumerations" give important clues to the meaning of "shall" in each statement and ultimately to the meaning of the entire statement. In case (3), a stipulation is made as to who shall possess "legislative Powers." The powers remain to be defined. In case (4), "Enumeration" is defined by the statement. We are informed about what kind of thing it is to be by the designation about when it is to be made. When "Powers" are defined, it is not in the same way since they are not the same kind of things as "Enumerations."

In case (4), a stipulation is placed on the "Enumeration" which refines and limits its meaning. "Shall" is used in a manner different in this case from the others. Case (3) is more like cases (1) and (2) than like case (4) in that it accords to "Congress" certain capacities. But case (3) differs from case (1) in that in case (1) a function is accorded which carries with it certain powers, while in case (3) general powers are accorded which delineate a role in the scheme of the Constitution. In the context of the Constitution, the first three cases designate more power by the stipulation. In the fourth case, the stipulation is a limitation on a previously defined entity.

In the following cases, the kind of things defined as "rights" differ, influencing the way in which each word "right" may be understood.

(5) . . . The *right* of the people to keep and bear arms, shall not be infringed.
(6) . . . The *right* of trial by jury shall be preserved . . . [Italics mine]

Here, the word is not joining different classes but is itself associated with different arrangements. Case (5) delineates a right of the people to do something. The "right" to keep and bear arms imposes a limitation on the government. This use of "right," in Hohfeld's scheme, designates a privilege which the government is not free to violate.[28] Case (6) specifies a right to have something done. The "right" to trial by jury is a right in the primary legal sense which Hohfeld suggests is synonymous with a claim. The government has a constitutional duty not to violate such a right.[29] The differences that exist are not found in the word "right," but are suggested by the kind of things associated with it in each case. Hohfeld's attempt to clear up legal usage is not unlike the therapeutic efforts made by general semanticists, discussed in Chapter 2. His formulation seeks greater clarity. However, Hohfeld's source for usage is in the language itself. His proposition is conceivable only because an indication of possible routes is to be found in conventional use. Richard Flathman develops this analysis further with greater sensitivity to the social basis for the meaning of words.[30] According to Flathman's scheme, "right" (5) is a "power" that the people have which the Constitution grants as an "immunity" from governmental intrusion.[31] "Right" (6) is a "liberty" which the state may not interfere with.[32] "Right" in each of these senses gets its meaning from the classes of words that it joins. In all its facets, it is a concept that has special meaning in the Constitution, a meaning which is examined further in the discussion of constitutional law as a language in Chapter 6.

The words "to keep and bear arms" differ from the words "trial by jury" in the senses just discussed because where the people may do the former without government intervention they cannot have the latter without its active involvement. This suggests one of the deep structural elements revealed by examining the meaning of words in context. The use of "shall" in association with bearing arms (5) emphasizes the way in which the constitutional scheme interacts with the larger social setting, and how action that is the product of this kind of relationship differs from (1-4) where the classes that are joined are totally constitutional constructs.

(B) DIFFERING SYNTACTICAL CONTEXTS

Syntactical contexts are the grammatical considerations which are often thought of as determining the meaning of statements. The term *grammar* is often used in this limited sense as designating the explicit rules for the use of language. In the present investigation, syntactical contexts are taken as descriptive of the way we use language rather than as prescriptive rules for correct usage. As such, they are merely one of the clues to meaning in language. When the word "shall" appears in different syntactical contacts, its meaning differs. For example:

(1) . . . an Inhabitant of that state in shich he *shall* be chosen.

(2) . . . the Electors in each state *shall* have the Qualifications requisite for electors of the most populous Branch of the State legislature.

(3) The House of Representatives *shall* chuse their speaker and other Officers; . . . [Italics mine]

In example (1), the auxiliary "shall" is used to express futurity. In example (2), "shall" expresses necessity. In example (3), "shall" is used to express compulsion. Here, the meaning also comes from the union of "shall" with the transitive verb "chuse," and the direct object completing the phrase. In each example, the meanings differ because of the syntactical contexts. As an auxiliary, "shall" is heavily dependent on the immediate context. The range of this sort of sensitivity extends from this case through words that are fully defined in the document, like "Senate" or "President," to those ordinary English words with a limited range of meanings, such as the age requirement for the President.

In the following examples, the meaning of another auxiliary verb, "may," is also suggested by the syntactical context.

(4) The President *may* require the Opinion, in writing, of the Principal Officer is each of the executive Departments . . .

(5) . . . one or the other Mode of Ratification *may* be proposed by Congress; . . . [Italics mine]

In sentence (4), "may" is used in the now archaic sense of "having the power to." This sense would presently be conveyed by "can," but the nature of the document is such that the ordinary distinction between permission to do something and the power to carry it out is meaningless.

In example (5), "may" expresses a contingency in a clause of result. "Mode of Ratification" is contingent upon what the Congress proposes. The nature of this contingent relation in the Constitution entails that the Congress has this power. As discussed in regard to example (4), the power is essential to this contingency. But in example (5) the contingency is dependent on the clause of result which relates the contingency to the stated possibilities.

Two very different meanings of the word "provided" are evident as a result of the syntactical context in these two examples.

(6) He shall have Power, by and with the Advice and Consent of the Senate, to make Treaties, *provided* two thirds of the Senators present concur; . . .
(7) and he shall nominate, and by and with the Advice and Consent of the Senate, shall appoint Ambassadors, other public ministers and Consuls, Judges of the Supreme Court, and all other Officers of the United States, whose Appointments are not herein otherwise *provided* for, . . . [Italics mine]

In these cases, syntax reveals the form of the word and hence what it is to mean. In case (6), "provided" is the past participle used as a conjunction and means "if." In case (7), "provided" is the past tense of the verb used intransitively to mean "stipulated." Word forms and syntax, which in these cases reveals the form, designate some of the more obvious and readily understood ways in which what is meant is contained in the language.

As a constituting instrument, the Constitution laid the contractual foundation from which the legitimacy of its functions developed. The development of political traditions in the United States, with reference to the Constitution, is part of the grammar that will subsequently be seen as constituting the "form of life" which is the basis for a view of constitutional law as a language. With attention here to syntax, the emphasis is still in the initial structural relations as they lay the foundation for future developments. That there has been little debate over these examples, in spite of the significance of the arrangements they stipulate, is an indication of the extent to which agreement on the use of language precludes the sort of controversy that seems to develop in its absence. Where the syntax contributes to clarity in meaning, the emerging political controversies of the day have no place to settle.

(C) DIFFERENT CRITERIA FOR SUBSTITUTION

The final and most abstract consideration for investigating the language in the Constitution, criteria for the appropriate substitution for words that appear synonymous, suggests the intuitive capacities which bear upon the use of language. These capacities reflect what the user of a language knows that will enable certain inferences to be made. Criteria for substitution involve the tacit conventions employed in interpreting and constructing sentences. Substitution is in some respects a catch-all approach to the examination of grammar. It includes the contextual (though not syntactical) considerations bearing on meaning; the tacit conventions which serve as intuitive clues to what makes sense; and the uses to which different categories of things can be put as a result of the relationships which we come to understand as we learn what constitutional law involves. In the following pairs of statements, words that might be substituted in one case are inappropriate as substitutes for the same word in the other context.

(1) . . . the executive thereof *may* make temporary Appointments until the next meeting of the legislature, . . .

(2) . . . at such Place or Places as the Congress *may* by law have directed. [Italics mine]

In case (1), the sense can be maintained by substitution of "is permitted to" or "is allowed to," but such a substitution in case (2) would alter the sense of the passage. The meaning is maintained by the substitution of "might," a substitution which would be inappropriate to case (1). In case (2), the capacity of Congress to act in this way is implicit. We know the meaning of the passage because the power is essential for the possibility that it be exercised. In case (1), a power is being granted, and thus the substitution is more specifically directed to the stipulation of that power. These powers and the contingent possibilities have been the subject of some controversy, not because of the ambiguity of the crucial word "may" but because the sense that dictates the appropriate substitution depends on the context of institutions and powers, which themselves are not given precise stipulation.

In another example, the word "shall" may again be seen to be
dependent on context, this time by examining appropriate substitutions.

(3) Every Bill . . . *shall*, before it becomes a law, be presented to the
    President.
(4) Every Bill which *shall* have passed the House of Representatives and the
    Senate, . . . [Italics mine]

It is appropriate to the meaning of case (3) to substitute "must" for
"shall." Such a substitution in case (4) would not be appropriate
because it would alter the meaning that the document is taken to
convey. "Shall," in case (3), presents a contingent possibility. It is
a requirement that a bill, as stated here, be presented to the President. In case (4), the requirement that a bill pass the two Houses of
Congress has already been stipulated, and here the meaning of
"shall" simply relies on that stipulation in stating a possible subsequent outcome. The author of the Constitution used "shall" on
exceedingly numerous occasions, and although the word has largely
been supplanted in ordinary English today by "will,"[33] the expressions in the Constitution have not lost their meaning. We understand nuances of meaning through substitution once we know the
nature of constitutional politics.

This chapter has discussed the nature of investigation into the
use of language. It has suggested the justification for such an investigation and the parameters which are recognized by philosophers of language as governing the investigation of language use.
The consideration of the language used in the Constitution has en-
deavored to show the utility and appropriateness of investigating
language for the meaning in the document. The discussion has
focused on sentences in the document. As has been proposed, there
is another level at which an investigation of language may proceed.
Such an investigation considers constitutional law as constituting a
unique language. Prior to moving to this level, in the next chapter I
discuss the aspects of modern linguistic theory which suggest its
utility for the study of constitutional interpretation.

NOTES

1. Harrison, *Meaning and Structure,* p. 4.

2. Stanley Cavell, *Must We Mean What We Say?* (New York: Charles Scribner's, 1969), p. 4.

3. Frederick Waismann, op. cit., p. 34.

4. Cavell, op. cit., p. 34.

5. Ludwig Wittgenstein, *On Certainty* (New York: Harper and Row, 1969), par. 124.

6. Ibid.

7. Wittgenstein, *Philosophical Investigations,* par. 241.

8. Wittgenstein, *On Certainty*, par. 613.

9. Hubert Schwyzer, "The Acquisition of Concepts and the Use of Language" (Ph.D. Dissertation, University of California, Berkeley, 1968), pp. 3–4.

10. Harrison, *Meaning and Structure*, p. 22.

11. Ibid., p. 231.

12. Wittgenstein, *Philosophical Investigations*, par. 81.

13. Stephen Toulmin, "Wittgenstein," *Encounter* 32 (1969): 69.

14. Waismann, op. cit., p. 13.

15. Ibid., p. 14.

16. Ibid., p. 102.

17. Wittgenstein, *Philosophical Investigations*, par. 85.

18. Ibid.

19. Ibid., par. 87.

20. Waismann, op. cit., p. 190.

21. Ibid.

22. *Palko v. Connecticut*, 302 U.S. 319 (1937).

23. *Rochin v. California*, 342 U.S. 165 (1952), is an obvious exception.

24. 302 U.S. 319 (1937).

25. *Adamson v. California*, 322 U.S. 46 (1947).

26. Ibid., Justice Black dissenting.

27. Waismann, op. cit, p. 189.

28. Wesley N. Hohfeld, *Fundamental Legal Conceptions* (New Haven, Conn.: Yale University Press, 1919), p. 39.

29. Ibid., p. 38.

30. Flathman, *The Practice of Rights.*

31. Ibid., pp. 37, 49.

32. Ibid., p. 39.

33. H. L. Mencken, *The American Language* (New York: Knopf, 1977), pp. 537–539.

5 | Meaning, Grammar, and Group Life

A model of language use based on the contemporary linguistic theories presented thus far and applied to law is an epistemologically unique approach to the activity of judging.[1] The model substantially alters what we can hope to understand and dictates a different focus for investigation. Consideration of interpretive behavior from a linguistic perspective facilitates rigorous analysis of substantively normative statements. Students of language have long recognized that even when they are observing metaphysical statements, "statements about the nature of these statements can be empirical."[2] In law, this means that what the judges have said is evidence for what their experience allows them to say. By this model, judicial decision depends on what it makes sense or seems appropriate to say about a given state of affairs. Sense, here, refers to convention and contextual understanding. The conventions in the law, operating at the highest appellate level, give meaning to discourse on constitutional issues and provide the ultimate constraints on how cases will be handled by those whose professional work is governed by legal language. In this way, the study of language shows how structural aspects operate on the interpretive process in constitutional law.

In the interest of developing such an analysis of constitutional law, this chapter argues for the derivation of meaning from the way groups use the language they share. The approach subsequently moves to a description of some important considerations bearing on the relation of language use to group life and the extent to which the model of a judicial role captures the significance of a unique language group.

MEANING AS USE

In his later work, Wittgenstein rejected the theory of language that has come to be associated with positivism and turned his attention to the characteristics of language in use.[3] Such attention resulted in the development of a theory of meaning based on practice. Wittgenstein's position is critical of the traditional thesis that meaning reflects an "objective" world. The life of the sign or word is not what it refers to but how it is used.[4] The theory is an alternative to the association of word to object that characterizes the empiricist theory. This theory of meaning is evident in the following passage: "Think of words as instruments characterized by their use, and then think of the use of a hammer, the use of a chisel, the use of a square, of a glue pot, and of the glue."[5] The observation suggests that we know a hammer when we know its use. A wooden stick with an irregular metal shape attached is of limited use until we understand at least some of the possibilities for putting it to work. Words are like this whether in ordinary language or in the Constitution. "Equal protection," for instance, has a rich, if imprecise, meaning in the history of constitutional law. Here, ordinary English can make some sense of the words, but a derivation from ordinary use is related to the constitutional concept, much as using a wooden hammer for a piece of kindling is related to using the tool for pounding a nail.

In his lectures, Wittgenstein was attentive to the differences between this view and the empiricist position. He described the comparison of language to a "calculus proceeding according to strict rules" as "one-sided" since such use was rare.[6] We do not ordinarily think of such rules, nor can native speakers bring to mind rules for ordinary use. Thus, he proposed that there is no separate meaning apart from use.

We are unable clearly to circumscribe the concepts we use; not because we don't know their real definition, but because there is no real "definition" to them. To suppose that there must be would be like supposing that whenever children play with a ball they play a game according to strict rules.[7]

Wittgenstein saw a "common mistake" in the empiricist theory: it was the impression that concepts have meaning apart from their use. This mistake is evident in the attempts to create precision in law by bringing words closer to the objects they are said to represent or to rules for use as discussed in Chapter 2. While lawyers and judges may be well advised to seek precision, the epistemological position that views meaning as dependent on rules or referents detracts from a capacity to explain both the nature of the constraints on Supreme Court Justices and the extent to which their use of the constitutional tradition as a basis for their opinions explains a unique aspect of their activity.

This position is amplified in *Philosophical Investigations*, where Wittgenstein describes language as being more akin to a model of action than to a "countersign of thought." The position is the result of an effort to free philosophy from conceptual confusion. It is based on Wittgenstein's belief that such confusion has resulted from the speculative and abstract nature of philosophical inquiries. This view, stressing as it does the qualities of language at work, has been called the use theory of meaning.

Gilbert Ryle, one of the Oxford school of ordinary language philosophers, suggests:

The famous saying: "Don't ask for the meaning, ask for use," . . . advised philosophers to switch their attention from the trouble-making words in their dormancy as language-pieces or dictionary items to their utilizations in the actual saying of things—from these words *qua* units of language to their live sentences in which they are being actively employed.[8]

The description of linguistic activity in terms of use belies the attempt to grasp an inner essence of meaning, proposing instead that we "look and see" how linguistic concepts are used.

Language is learned by examples. These are not examples of some*thing*, but are guides for how we ought to speak if we wish to be understood. In using language, competent speakers are able to perform operations of which they may not be aware. The exploration of constitutional language is based on the proposition that use does not have to follow past practices as if they were rules. Rather, the use that is made of language may be a basis for descriptive rules developed in the effort to understand existing practices. Authority is a characteristic of rules that is largely absent in the constitutional setting when the rules are made by the Supreme Court. Although this is less true where an existing group of Justices gives special weight to a decision of their predecessors, this kind of authority is merely a case of conventional use which is buttressed by a sense of judicial role. (Further discussion of role theory and its relation to linguistic conventions concludes this chapter.) This dimension of judicial decision is minimized here in order to state the stronger and less often considered case of constraints operating in addition to the strength of authority. Since past opinions constitute possible forms of action as well as norms, they are essential to the description of constitutional law as a language. Where the Justices are influenced by prior examples as guides to action, they are subject to the requirements of intelligible communication.

The Justices of the Supreme Court are certainly more concerned than ordinary speakers of a language with attaching their decisions to past actions. To know the language of constitutional law is to be able to describe the prior uses which are internalized in ordinary language.[9] However, it is implicit in the comparison suggested here that the recitation of prior cases in decisions of the Supreme Court is an activity that follows, and in many ways may be distinguished, from the intellectual process leading up to a decision. In the judicial context, the Justices have learned that certain ways of doing things are appropriate or reasonable. This is in the nature of linguistic constraints, whether in the ordinary context or in that of the Constitution. Examples of this dimension of symbolic activity are more fully developed in the ordinary context than in law. As Wittgenstein has argued, "humans who employ such a concept as fear would not have to be able to describe its use. And were they to try, it is possible that they would give a quite inadequate description (like most people, if they tried to describe money correctly)."[10] Whether an individual speaker can describe what he is doing with language is irrelevant to this theory. The speaker learns language by learning to use words in certain ways. Because this skill is not generally acquired through a process of analysis or description, it is not surprising that we should find it difficult to describe what we have learned. It is important that in knowing a language one knows how to do certain things, whether or not they can be described.

The linguistic devices basic to language use are learned by

examples and practice. These examples are the key to meaning: "If a person has not yet got the concepts, I shall teach him to use the words by means of examples and by practice.—And when I do this I do not communicate less to him than I know myself."[11] The investigation of the learning process and the nature of the linguistic devices are, as far as the present work is concerned, the study of language proposed in steps toward the description of meaningfulness. A view of the learning process in law on the basis of this theory is considered in Chapter 7. The learning process discussed here suggests that there is no essence of meaning.

One of the cases in which Wittgenstein explains the use of language in novel situations demonstrates the futility of looking for some essence that is more "real" than the use of language itself. He refers to a case in which a teacher presents a pupil with a sequence of numbers such as 994, 996, 998, and 1,000, and tells the pupil to "go on." The case represents the situation in language where the speaker applies what he has learned to a novel context: ". . . it seems to us as though in this case the instructor imparted the meaning to the pupil—without telling him it directly; but in the end the pupil is brought to the point of giving himself the correct ostensive definition. And there is where the illusion is."[12] When new sentences are formulated in language, the speaker must decide how to "go on" relative to what his experience indicates. The examples that teach how to "go on" are thus the core of meaning. Such a procedure, as is evident in this example, may be described in terms of a formulation such as "counting by twos." But such a formula is nothing more than our shorthand explanation of what is suggested by the conventions. The examples are all there is, even though the name "counting by twos" may be given to the concept derived from the examples.

The meaning of privacy in the constitutional setting has been derived from examples of action by the Supreme Court. The examples, revealing protections accorded to personal, marital, familial, and sexual privacy comprise the meaning of the right. Clearly, it is not some essence that gives meaning to the concept. Rather, judicial opinions marshal the evidence, the prior examples that convey "the concept of personal 'liberty' embodied in the Fourteenth Amendment's Due Process Clause." By referring to actions on the First, Fourth, and Fifth Amendments and to the "penumbras" of the Bill of Rights,[13] the Justices have fashioned a meaningful concept on the basis of prior use. Thus, even the explicit discussion of the law in judicial opinion operates on the same principle as ordinary language—that use is the bedrock of meaning.

Clarifying the position that the activity of language use is central to the search for meaning, ordinary language philosophers have attempted to do away with the search for some third thing that two words having the same meaning share. J.F.M. Hunter, for instance, concentrates on the following passage in the *Investigations:* "For a large class of cases—though not for all—in which we employ the word meaning it can be defined thus: the meaning of a word is its use in the language."[14] Hunter proposes that this passage be understood to say that "has the same use as" may be substituted for any form of the word "mean."[15] There is no essential meaning separate from or more fundamental than the resemblances derived from particular cases. According to Hunter, it is not required to read the expression "have the same meaning" in such a way that it gives rise to questions about what that meaning is. Since this theory eliminates the search for more "real" referents than the words themselves, it is an alternative not only to the empiricist theory, but also to the explanation of symbolic processes and the discussion of their behavioral significance. This holds true especially as such explanations have generally depended on a positivist foundation.

A notion of law, apart from the way law is used, i.e., the way things are referred to in law, makes no sense. Since the reference to things in constitutional law is basically a linguistic activity, meaning in constitutional law can only exist as a result of the way the concepts, principles, and maxims that constitute this tradition are used. Since meaning in language cannot be understood apart from use, the linguistic aspects of legal interpretation can also be explained in terms of use in such a way that "what the judges say" does not imply either more "real" or less "legal" activity. If meaning in language can only be understood in terms of prior examples and the conceptual possibilities they reveal, then the same may be true of constitutional law.

GRAMMAR AND GROUP LIFE

Wittgenstein began his *Philosophical Investigations* with a criticism of the view that language is learned by ostensive definition, which is the basis of language acquisition in the empiricist theory. He proposes that ostensive definition does not explain an important aspect of what it is to know a language, i.e., the conceptual abilities which enable words to be used in meaningful constructions. According to Wittgenstein, the key to language acquisition is learning not merely the right word for an object, but the entire concept to which the object-word applies.[16] The uses of the word make up the concept and suggest its role in the language. An understanding of this role is postulated as a prerequisite to defining a word. The role is learned when what it is appropriate to do with the concept is understood.

Language learning, according to Wittgenstein, involves a complicated dialectic rather than the processes of inductive generalization and ostensive definition in the empiricist theory. Since there is no essential meaning which words reflect, the meaning must lie in the different uses experienced by the speakers.[17] In acquiring this experience, while learning language, we learn language and the world together.[18] For example, the limitations on the theory of ostensive definition lie in the fact that things can be defined for use only if we already understand something of how the definition is to be taken. Wittgenstein puts it this way: "If I know that someone means to explain a color-word to me, the ostensive definition 'that is called sepia' will help me to understand the word."[19] Ostensive definition explains part of how we come to acquire language, but it is not the most important part. It is not the process which should be taken as characteristic of language.

In ordinary language philosophy, the knowledge of concepts is more fundamental to the nature of language than the ostensive definition of object words. Knowledge of the meaning of concepts is acquired when one learns how to use them. It is only when we "know how to use the word 'anger' that we know what anger is."[20] The way in which concepts are acquired is elaborated in *On Certainty*, Wittgenstein's investigations into the problems of what we can know. He suggests that "children do not learn that books exist, that armchairs exist, etc., etc., etc.,—they learn to fetch books, sit in armchairs, etc., etc.''[21] This example suggests another way of demonstrating the importance of use in the acquisition of meaning; it indicates the way in which the practices that we conceptualize function in a language. These practices are the basis of the grammar of our language.

Wittgenstein proposes that grammar, conceived in this way, is fundamental to our conceptual structure and hence to meaning. His statements of this principle are obscure, but, given the greater familiarity of the empiricist tradition, Wittgenstein's entire position often seems that way. Yet, this principle is of such potential significance that it is worth considering carefully. With references to grammar, he states that "essence is expressed by grammar.[22] Grammar tells what kind of object anything is.''[23] As a key to meaning, grammar represents basic linguistic competence. It is through the grammar of our language that we know the world. Grammar governs the "possibilities of phenomena" and regulates the "kind of statement that we make.''[24] What enables the users of language to make judgments about the correctness of what can be said is that words have a certain grammar.[25] Although dependent on experience, "grammar" is logically prior to any given instance of language use; hence, it depicts how we understand our experience.[26]

This interpretation of the relationship between language and the world is the basis for the claim that modern linguistic theory presents a new epistemological position. Since we learn language and the world together, it is not the "world" which gives meaning to our language. We understand the world in terms of the language through which it is revealed. Grammar tells how the world is to be seen. We may want to say that the world exists apart from language, but, given the significance of our language for the view we have of that world, the nature of such a "real" world is less consequential than the way in which we come to conceptualize our world.

One of the main sources of Wittgenstein's theory of grammar is the *Blue and Brown Books*. There, he is "concerned with the grammar of those words which describe what are called 'mental activities:' seeing, hearing, feeling, etc. and this comes to the same

as saying that we are concerned with the grammar of 'phrases concerning sense data.'"[27] The interpretation of the relation of
language to sense data develops the proposition that language is the
basis for the world as we know it. When we say that we "see" a
body, the grammar of the language activity suggests that we are
"pointing to the *appearance* of a body."[28] The "grammar" of
seeing suggests that "seeing" means pointing to sense data.
Language determines what it means "to see," not what is in view or
the capacity of our eyes.

Meaning is not merely a reflection of the sense data which
language has been presumed to mirror. The meaning of language is
contained in its grammar.

It is part of the grammar of the word "chair" that this is what we call "to
sit on a chair," and it is part of the grammar of the word "meaning" that
this is what we call "explanation of a meaning;" in the same way to explain
my criterion for another person's having a toothache is to give a grammatical explanation about the word "toothache" and, in this sense, an
explanation concerning the meaning of the word "toothache."[29]

What is learned when one learns what Wittgenstein calls the "role"
of an activity in the lives of those for whom it is a practice is the
grammar of the activity. The acquisition of the grammar of words,
concepts, and activities enables the person learning a language to
employ definitions.

In this context, in order to learn the word "chess" one must first
acquire a knowledge of what games are; in order to learn the word
"Mass" one must learn what religious ceremonies are. What makes
chess one kind of activity and saying Mass another is that they have
different grammars. In this regard, grammar "is a matter of what
sorts of things are relevant, appropriate, make sense to say" in
regard to these activities.[30] It is appropriate to ask who won or is
winning at chess but not at Mass.

In considering the limits bearing on grammar, ordinary language
philosophers sometimes attempt to consider the grammar rather
than the rules of language because of the limitations of the traditional notion of rules for the description of language. The
grammar of a situation is a consideration more basic than its rules.

Grammar, rather than rules, determines what can be said about a situation. The importance of grammar and the difference between grammar and rules are developed in an article by Hubert Schwyzer.[31] Schwyzer describes what appears to be a chess game. The game is played by the rules traditionally associated with chess, but it is performed by priests in a foreign land to determine the will of the gods. Schwyzer argues against the contentions of Searle and Rawls[32] that the rules of chess, by creating and defining a form of behavior, define the nature of chess-playing and tell what kind of thing chess-playing is.[33] Schwyzer's position is that the Austinian tradition confuses the rules of an activity with what Wittgenstein calls its "grammar."[34] "What makes chess-playing the kind of thing it is is a matter of what sorts of things it makes sense to say with respect to chess."[35] Grammar, in the sense proposed by Wittgenstein, can here be seen as "the 'role' of the activity in the lives of those for whom it is a practice."[36]

The relation of the conventions that constitute our grammar to the formulations of rules or codes to clarify the conventions is brought out by Stanley Cavell:

Establishing a norm is not telling us how we ought to perform an action, but telling us how that action is done, or how it is to be done. Contrariwise, telling us what we ought to do is not instituting a norm to cover the case, but rather presupposes that there is something to do which it would be correct to do.[37]

Conventional activity has established ways of proceeding. When these ways are regular and predictable, rules can be formulated to describe them. Some activity is, of course, regularized by the rules, as for instance professional football. It is hard to imagine this form of activity without rules. Yet, before it reached its present heights there were games of football played with far less reliance on rules. Constitutional law suggests a reversal of this evolutionary scheme. There were rules as a basis for this activity and the activity itself laid down the rules. But on the Supreme Court, the process of interpreting the Constitution is more like a conventional activity in language because of the absence of an authoritative statement as to how to proceed. The nature of these conventions can profit by further investigation of the characteristics of linguistic convention. Wittgenstein refers to our knowledge of language in terms of "language games." In an activity such as football, one can play without knowing the rules. More often than not, games are learned not by acquiring the rules and then following them, but by setting out to play. Language is composed of practices governed by a series of relationships rather than by rules. By describing how we put words together in this way, ordinary language philosophy presents a model of language developed out of use rather than on the basis of prescriptive rules.

Instead of producing something common to all that we call language, I am saying that these phenomena have no one thing in common . . . but they are related to one another in different ways. And it is because of this relationship, or these relationships, that we call them all "language."[38]

Wittgenstein proposes that the instances that are called "language," or the uses of language, should be understood as forming a family. The features of related situations in language use, the "network of partially overlapping similarities," he calls "family resemblances."[39]

The description of language use suggests that language is composed of games or sets of "family resemblances." Knowledge of these games is one of the elements of a linguistic capacity and is the result of shared experience. A common experience with language in use is the basis of the capacity to communicate with language. In the case of seeing a color and reporting it, a "successful" report is a result not just of relating a word to a color, but of *knowing what it is to correctly apply a color word*. For this to count as a linguistic operation, i.e., an operation which is part of a language, there must be shared conventions.[40] For the operation to be part of a language we must know the application, in the sense of being aware of the convention.

As a basis for considering the linguistic dimensions of constitutional interpretation, it is necessary to elaborate briefly the significance of the conventional structures or forms of life for language. For Wittgenstein, "To imagine a language means to imagine a form of life."[41] "What has to be accepted, the given is—so one could say—forms of life."[42] The description of a "form of life" looks to what is common in an activity that allows communication. For communication there must be a basis of agreement.

The discussion in this chapter of the meaning of words and the grammar of constitutional law has shown that there are accepted conventions evident in the language of the document. These conventions are evident in the way we use the words and the language of the Constitution. In the next chapter, they will be shown to be implicit in the way the document is interpreted.

To be part of a system of communication, it must be possible to correlate utterances with conventions that have a social basis. Farhang Zabeeh explicitly states this requirement in proposing that "if we sever an utterance from its particular conditions and use it under any conditions or a condition which does not belong to it, we may produce nonsense."[43] The language of constitutional law, if it is used, depends on the traditional formulations which are learned when the language is learned. Such a requirement would not reveal the outcome of a particular case, but it limits how an appeal or an opinion might be formulated.

Ordinary language philosophy suggests that an investigation of correctness is inappropriate to linguistic analysis. There is no clear line of the sensible by which correctness can be judged. Asking for "correctness" suggests a view of language rooted in a calculus. Such a view is erroneous because it is like asking if we are "correct" or justified in being what we are.[44] What is essential is merely the recognition that to be part of a language, an utterance must make sense. Knowing the grammar of an expression is knowing "criteria" for use of the expression, i.e., when and why it makes sense.

In Wittgenstein's *Blue and Brown Books*, the regularities of grammar which bind diverse phenomena together are called conventions. In *Philosophical Investigations*, the term *"convention"* is replaced by "form of life."[45] A "form of life" is the source of conventions, and conventions are what make communication possible. The conceptualizations that make communication possible are evident in language, and they depend on group life.[46]

The relation of concepts to generalizations suggests the importance of grammar to understanding the world. It is quite common to suppose that knowing a generalization enables one to grasp a concept. This would be something like knowing that there is more than one kind of chair and that a particular thing can be called a chair because we know the general classification. Ordinary language philosophy reverses this explanation of the learning process: "One cannot explain what concepts are in terms of the notion of generalization. People do not first make generalizations and then embody them in concepts; it is only by virtue of their possession of concepts that they are able to make generalizations at all."[47] This sense of the nature of grammar and its place in a theory of language are the basis for the description of law as language. As is elaborated in the following chapter, it is the unique grammar of constitutional law which allows it to be considered a language. Such a consideration allows the judicial decision to be viewed in terms of linguistic interpretation.

Meaning and grammar are functional aspects of language which show how language analysis may contribute to the understanding of legal interpretation. Linguistic analysis suggests that, in the study of legal interpretation, we should look to how the language of law is used. This position is based on a different theory of knowledge than that which has set the parameters for investigating judicial behavior. The modern linguistic theory of grammar emphasizes the importance of the acquisition of concepts and the role of these concepts in the lives of those who use them. It further suggests that these concepts are tied to the group life from which they emerge. The sphere of activity which employs the language of constitutional law will be considered such a "form of life."

DESCRIBING GROUP LIFE

By relating language to "group life," this theory of meaning suggests the attempt, in the study of politics, to relate group expectations to individual action through a theory of "judicial role." Discussion of this theory, with attention to its limits in expressing meaning, is as close as public law scholarship has come to investigating the significance of group practices in the judicial decision. The formulation does not quite fit as a basis for amplifying a Wittgensteinian notion of a form of life, but it is sufficiently close to merit attention here. Its limitations simply indicate some of the respects in which the discussion of language improves on this closely related framework.

Investigation of a "judicial role"—the judge's view of what is expected of him—was first suggested as an intervening variable in the judicial response to the stimuli of a particular case by Pritchett in *The Roosevelt Court*[48] and was developed in his *Civil Liberties and the Vinson Court*.[49] The variable has been employed more recently by Theodore L. Becker and others.[50] Some limitations emerge in Becker's formulation of the concept of judicial role when compared with the examination of judicial interpretation from a linguistic perspective. Becker's work concentrates on the personal or psychological aspects of role perception, and as such he is operating in the realm of interpretation which has been the main focus of this study. Many other interesting studies of the operation of the judicial role are not considered here because sufficient grounds for comparison of linguistic analysis and role theory can be found in Becker's position.

Becker has been critical of judicial behavioralists like Schubert[51] who believe that they have "debunked" the impact of substantive law on the judicial decision. However, he recognizes that the following argument has been subjected to serious attack: "That the Law was a body of general rules (major premise) from which, by a process of deduction (after the introduction of a minor premise) any specific controversy could be correctly solved through arriving at a more specific rule which would determine the proper immediate solution."[52] Becker believes that this argument is based substantially in natural law beliefs, i.e., the idea that the common law is "the perfection of reason"—a body of rules acquiring a sort of transcendental existence.[53] Becker has attempted to show, in a fashion consistent with behavioralism, how such a conception of law might have an impact on the judicial decision.

Certainly a judge's own perception of how he should operate is important to the description of his activity. In a study of judicial role, Kenneth Vines classifies judicial respondents as law interpreters, lawmakers, and pragmatists.[54] As Becker has pointed out, the Vines study "circumvents the issue of whether the judicial role constrained the preexistent personal attitudes of the judges."[55] Although this is clearly beyond what Vines sets out to do, Becker's position raises the crucial issue for the analysis of judicial decision within the political process. Becker attempts to document the impact of law on the decision. This goal may be achieved more dramatically by transcending the positivist epistemology through the linguistic model with its conception of a shared body of conventions.

Becker argues that the jurisprudential "exhortation to the occupant" of the judicial position is a norm porposed by legal scholars as a desirable type of decision-making.[56] However, jurisprudence does not explain what Becker would like to know, i.e., whether or not precedent actually operates this way in the judicial process. Becker wants to show that it does. His definition of a court requires that the role considerations, which he is interested in revealing, actually affect a judicial decision. By definition, he considers a court

(1) a man or body of men (2) with power to decide a dispute (3) before whom the parties or advocates or their surrogates present the facts of the dispute and cite existent, expressed, primary normative principles that (4) are applied by that man or those men (5) who *believe* that they should listen to the presentation of facts and apply such cited normative principles impartially, objectively, or with detachment, and (6) that they may so decide, and (7) as an independent body.[57]

Becker's theory emerges from a jurisprudential proposition as to how courts ought to function. His investigation pursues whether or not it actually does function in the prescribed way.

In methodological terms, Becker equates the judicial role with the "delegate" role as explicated in *The Legislative System*.[58] The "delegate" role is akin to "the notion of personal value impartiality or objectivity which we have earmarked as the chief theoretically distinguishing characteristic between the judicial process and all other policy making processes."[59] The judge is compared to the delegate in his impartiality. In the judicial setting, this impartiality is the result of "the dictates of relevant law" limiting substantive value preferences.[60] The legislative "delegate" is characterized by the degree to which his personal value preferences are submerged in favor of constituent pressures. According to Becker, the judge feels the press of role as the relevance of a case or rule becomes clear.[61] Thus, the judicial role is characterized as being (1) objective in that the substantive value preferences of the judges are not involved, and (2) precedent-oriented in that "established, relevant, clear legal precedent"[62] determines the decision.

Becker employs survey research to substantiate his hypothesis of a unique judicial role and reports that the judicial role is assumed more often by those trained in the law than by those with no law school training.[63] These findings, in Becker's opinion, afford some evidence for the existence of a judicial role explained in part as precedent orientation.[64] Thus, the search for evidence of a judicial role stems from the common law traditions of *stare decisis* as a unique characteristic of the law, and it is operationalized as "precedent orientation."

A number of students of the legal process have pointed out the limitations of the "precedent orientation" concept. Since, at the appellate level, precedents quite often exist on either side of a controversy, the concept has been said to be empirically weak.[65] Martin Shapiro has cited the widespread misunderstanding of "precedent orientation,"[66] and Francis Rich concurs with the view that there is considerable lack of clarity in the use of the term.[67] Rich sees "precedent orientation" as an element of the judicial role. Shapiro, however, attempts to redefine a theory of *stare decisis* by means of a communications approach to the judicial opinion.[68] This position reflects some of the basic concepts of the linguistic model presented in this volume.

In reacting to the supposed debunking of the role of legal principles in the judicial decision, Becker turned to precedent in order to resurrect these principles. Yet, the limitations of the concept forced him to step back slightly. In a recent redefinition of his concept of the judicial role, Becker slacks off from his original position. However, he continues to maintain a positivistic conception similar to the one associated with the empiricist theory of language. His work assumes that there is law "out there" which is connected to the behavior of judges only by their perception of a role that commands them to follow precedent.

In his later work, Becker expresses concern that his conceptualization may indeed be too limited in that "expectations concerning a strict adherence by judges to norms are no longer sure to be fulfilled."[69] He substitutes "law oriented" for "precedent oriented,"[70] concluding that he is looking merely for the "judicial factor" in the judicial role—the restraint on personal values that gives the judicial role its "peculiar flavor."[71] As restated, restraint depends on a notion of objectivity and impartiality under law.

Whether the judge can be said to be bound to the law, in the sense of following what has been laid down at the expense of his own personal values, has certainly never been proven. The contribution of the study of law as a language is that the judge is seen to possess certain skills—he knows the law as a tool. Law is not something he can take up one day and ignore the next. Although it is a tool with multiple uses, it cannot accommodate any or all uses. The language of the law orders the judge's view of the world. The idea of impartiality is thus as problematic as precedent orientation when compared with a linguistic theory of the legal decision. The general limitation, then, of Becker's position is that it perpetuates a dichotomy between law and behavior in the legal process. He seeks an intervening variable as a link which would direct the judge to behave in a certain way. Law is viewed as having an impact on the behavior of judges because the judge perceives his role as dictating that he should follow the law as it has been laid down.

Julius Stone suggests the position proposed in this study: "In order to approach . . . the role of the appellate judge in law, creation, and development, we must first reconnoiter and traverse . . . the terrain of language. . . ."[72] The study of law as a language holds that, rather than sticking to precedent, the measure of the law's impact on behavior should be the ability to operate with the unique language of constitutional law. It is the linguistic capacities of those trained in law and the forum which depends on those capacities which make judicial decision-making a special kind of political activity.

Pritchett's earlier foundation is a good deal more subtle, and it is one to which the linguistic model can be more readily applied. Rather than proposing that the uniqueness of the judiciary rests in an impartial adherence to precedent, Pritchett wrote:

The individual judges may think that the precedents are wrong or out-moded. If so, he may follow his personal preferences and state his reasons for voting to change the Law. He is free to do that. He is not free to ignore the precedents, to act as though they did not exist. He has free choice, but among limited alternatives.[73]

From the perspective of linguistic theory, one reason the choices are limited is that they must be intelligible, and our language governs what makes sense. Judges cannot ignore the basic gram-matical aspects of the tradition because it is by means of these aspects of legal language that they have come to understand con-stitutional law. The theory of meaning proposed in the beginning of this chapter is a foundation for a description akin to that of the judicial role where grammar and "forms of life" become the iden-tity for the range of possibilities open to a Justice.

NOTES

1. F.S.C. Northrup, "Law, Language and Morals," *Yale Law Journal* 71 (May 1962), p. 1017.

2. Kenneth Burke, *A Grammar of Motives* (New York: Prentice-Hall, 1945), pp. 57–58.

3. Ludwig Wittgenstein, *Blue and Brown Books* (New York: Harper and Row, 1964).

4. Ibid., p. 4.

5. Ibid., p. 67.

6. Ibid., p. 25.

7. Ibid.

8. Gilbert Ryle, "Use, Usage and Meaning," *Proceedings of the Aris-totelian Society*, Suppl. Vol. 35 (1961), pp. 223–230.

9. Wittgenstein, *Philosophical Investigations*, par. 114.

10. Ibid., par. 525.

11. Ibid., par. 208.

12. Ibid., par. 362.

13. *Roe v. Wade,* op. cit.

14. Wittgenstein, *Philosophical Investigations,* par. 43.

15. J.F.M. Hunter, "Wittgenstein on Meaning and Use," in *Essays on Wittgenstein*, ed. E. D. Klemke (Urbana, Ill.: University of Illinois Press, 1971), p. 382.

16. Hannah Pitkin, op. cit., p. 34.

17. Wittgenstein, *Philosophical Investigations,* par. 532.

18. Cavell, op. cit., p. 19.

19. Wittgenstein, *Philosophical Investigations*, op. cit., par. 30.

20. Stanley Cavell, "The Claim to Rationality" (Ph.D. Dissertation, Harvard University, 1961–1962), p. 227.

21. Wittgenstein, *On Certainty*, par. 476.

22. Ibid., par. 371.

23. Ibid., par. 373.

24. Wittgenstein, *Philosophical Investigations,* par. 96, 97.

25. Ibid., par. 242, 261.

26. Pitkin, op. cit., p. 120.

27. Wittgenstein, *Blue and Brown Books,* p. 70.

28. Ibid., p. 71.

29. Ibid., p. 24.

30. Schwyzer, op. cit., pp. 106–107.

31. Hubert Schwyzer, "Rules and Practices," *Philosophical Review* (October 1969): 451–467.

32. John Searle, "What Is a Speech Act?" *Philosophy in America* (London, 1965); John Rawls, "Two Concepts of Rules," *Philosophical Review* 64 (1955):3–32.

33. Schwyzer, "Rules," p. 455.

34. Wittgenstein, *Philosophical Investigations,* par. 371, 373.

35. Schwyzer, "Rules," p. 454.

36. Ibid., p. 464.

37. Cavell, *Must We Mean What We Say?*, p. 21.

38. Wittgenstein, *Philosophical Investigations,* par. 65.

39. Ibid., par. 66–69, 75.

40. Wittgenstein, "Notes for Lectures on 'Private Experience' and 'Sense Data,'"*Philosophical Review* 77 (1968). Reprinted in *Introduction to the Philosophy of Mind,* ed. Harold Morick (Glenview, Ill.: Scott, Foresman, 1920), pp. 155–194.

41. *Philosophical Investigations*, par. 19.

42. Ibid., par. 221.

43. Farhang Zabeeh, "On Language Games and Forms of Life," in Klemke, op. cit., p. 343.

44. Barry Stroud, "Wittgenstein and Logical Necessity," in Klemke, op. cit.

45. Wittgenstein, *Philosophical Investigations*, par. 182, 572–573.

46. Winch, op. cit.

47. Ibid.

48. Pritchett, *The Roosevelt Court.*

49. Pritchett, *Civil Liberties.*

50. For a bibliography, see Becker, *Comparative Judicial Politics,* Chapter 1; also Flango and Ducat, op. cit.

51. Schubert, "Judicial Attitudes and Voting Behavior."

52. Becker, *Political Behavioralism*, p. 42.

53. Ibid., pp. 42–43.

54. Vines, "The Judicial Role in American States," in Grossman and Tanenhaus, op. cit., pp. 461–488.

55. Becker, *Comparative Judicial Politics,* p. 57.

56. Ibid.

57. Ibid., p. 13.

58. John L. Wahlke, et al., *The Legislative System* (New York: John Wiley, 1962).

59. Becker, *Political Behavioralism*, p. 74.

60. Ibid., p. 67.

61. Ibid., p. 53.

62. Ibid., p. 99.

63. Becker, "A Survey of Hawaiian Judges: The Effect on Decisions of Judicial Role Variation," *American Political Science Review* 60 (September 1966):680.

64. Ibid.

65. C. Herman Pritchett, "The Development of Judicial Research," in Grossman and Tanenhaus, p. 31. See also Thomas A. Cowan, "Decision Theory in Law, Science and Technology," *Rutgers Law Review* 17 (1963): 499.

66. Martin Shapiro, "Political Jurisprudence," *Kentucky Law Journal* 55 (1963–1964): 294–343.

67. Francis M. Rich, Jr., "Role Perception and Precedent Orientation as Variables Influencing Appellate Judicial Decision Making: An Analysis of the Fifth Circuit Court of Appeals" (Ph.D. Dissertation, University of Georgia, 1967), p. 24.

68. Martin Shapiro, "Toward a Theory of Stare Decisis," *Journal of Legal Studies* 1 (January 1972):125.

69. Becker, *Comparative Judicial Politics*, p. 35.

70. Ibid.

71. Ibid.

72. Stone, *Law and the Social Sciences in the Second Half Century* (Minneapolis: University of Minnesota Press, 1966), p. 56.

73. Pritchett, *Civil Liberties*, p. 187. See also W. Murphy and C. Herman Pritchett, *Courts, Judges and Politics: An Introduction to the Judicial Process* (New York: Random House, 1961), p. 10; Pritchett, *American Constitution*, p. 51.

6 | Constitutional Law as Language

On the basis of its grammar and unique practices, constitutional law may be described as a language and not simply as use of English in a particular setting. The grammatical relations that exist in the Constitution delineate a professional language which, at least at the highest appellate level, has the qualities of a "natural" rather than formal language. Practices exist in constitutional law whose sense is determined by the relations delineated in the Constitution and the spheres of activity on which it depends, law and politics. The discussion of the language in the Constitution in Chapter 4 demonstrates how the characteristics of the constitutional system are shown by the language used in the document. Grammar, as discussed here, carries the example of language a step further. It addresses conceptual structures unique to the Constitution and develops their significance for judicial decision. The grammar of constitutional language reveals social practices fundamental to the formulation of judicial opinions.

The language of constitutional law is a legal language. The special significance of the political relations in the Constitution shows the difference between the language of the Constitution and that of law generally. However, the difference between the language of the Constitution and legal language in general is less important to this investigation than the difference between ordinary English and this particular legal language. The ways in which the language of constitutional law differs from ordinary English are emphasized in this chapter.

Constitutional language involves grammatical relations which influence the way in which a particular constitutional question may be understood. Examples of the grammar of constitutional law which distinguish it from other spheres of language are evident in (1) legal practices such as the case or controversy requirement, the appellate process, the issue of retroactivity, and the legal guarantees of the Bill of Rights and (2) practices in the Constitution of a basically political nature such as "judicial review," the "commerce power," "search and seizure," and "privacy."

GRAMMAR AND LANGUAGE

Traditionally, legal language has meant the vocabulary and rhetoric which are unique to the legal sphere. In 1949, Frederick Philbrick, in *Language and the Law*, addressed what he saw as a problem of word meanings in law. His thesis was essentially that law uses too many abstract words. This perspective is representative of the examination of language and law in the discussion of the empiricist theory in Chapter 2. In his more recent work, Mellinkoff concentrates on describing the vocabulary and forms which the law employs. He relates the development and use of the words and phrases employed by lawyers and judges, and he also considers the contribution of these words and phrases to some generally agreed-upon legal goals.[1] These works have not described law as language in the sense, so important to the modern study of language, of having a grammar of its own. For constitutional law to be considered a language and not merely an activity with a technical vocabulary, it must have a grammar dependent upon the existence of unique practices. A description of these practices is the goal of this chapter.

In examining linguistic theory in the previous chapters, it was shown that the important consideration for how we come to acquire a language is learning not merely the definitions of words but also their role in the lives of those who use them. This important insight of ordinary language philosophy distinguishes the description of language proposed by this school from positivist or empiricist theories. The existence of such grammatical relations in constitutional law is the key to the claim that this body of tradition can be treated as a language. It is possible to know an ordinary English approximation of such constitutional concepts as "interstate commerce" or "equal protection" without knowing the constitutional tradition. Without knowing that tradition, however, it would be impossible to begin to use these concepts in an appeal to the Justices of the Supreme Court. As has been demonstrated with regard to linguistic theory, knowledge of the meaning of a word depends on knowing its use. Although we can get clues to the use of a word from a dictionary, perhaps to fill in gaps in our training, we cannot get the use from a dictionary. This is the basis for Cavell's proposal that looking up a word in a dictionary is the *final* stage of learning a language.[2] Descriptions of legal vocabulary and of legal forms no more get at what is central to language than ostensive definition of diagrammed sentences tell what a language is.

Similarly, checking a precedent through reference to the numerous resources available to the lawyer or Justice must be considered the last stage of the process of formulating an opinion. This task, which is often left up to the clerks in the Supreme Court, is a process that follows rather than precedes the conceptualization of a particular issue as falling in a certain tradition of use. Whether in consideration of a petition for *certiorari* or in the formulation of an opinion of the Court, the resort to reference material can only fill in the gaps. It can only refine the final judicial product and is not appropriately considered the basis for the decision. It is in order to support this contention that constitutional language is seen as based in the unique conceptual factors rather than in the vocabulary. If the process were merely one of looking up precedent, then of course, there would be no difference in the decision-making capacities and propensities of a layman and a judge trained in the law. The fact that all Justices of the Supreme Court have been trained in the law has meant that the decisions they render are different from those that would be rendered by lay magistrates.

On the basis of the significance of grammar, the student of judicial decision can begin to examine the important distinction between the rules which delineate conventional procedures and the established linguistic practices which are fundamental to these procedures. There is an important difference between a statement that a claim in law has a poor chance of being ruled on favorably and a statement that a claim makes not sense at all, i.e., that it is unintelligible.[3] The difference exists because some aspects of practices or concepts can be designated by rules, while the role of these practices or concepts in our lives, i.e., the kind of practices which they are, depends on grammar.

The difference between rules and grammar demonstrates the importance of unique practices in legal relations. As mentioned in the previous chapter, Schwyzer explains this difference in addressing himself to claims which he feels confuse "the rules of an activity of a given kind with what Wittgenstein calls the 'grammar' of an activity, which makes it an activity of that kind."[4] Thus, it would be wrong to say that the activity of playing chess is constituted by action in accordance with its rules, or that the rules define that activity.[5] This is the case because understanding what it is to play a game is more fundamental to the activity of playing chess than any of the rules for correct play.

According to Schwyzer, christening a ship and making a will constitute conventionalized procedures rather than practices.[6] Ordinary language philosophers have not always recognized this distinction.[7] More fundamental than christening a ship is the concept of *giving a name to a ship* in our language. That which is appropriate to naming a ship is essential to the concept of christening while all that may be required by the rules of christening need not necessarily be applied to the naming of a ship. In like manner, *bequeathing* is the practice in relation to which making a will is the legal or conventional procedure. Giving a name to a ship and bequeathing are their own point.[8] *Giving a name to a ship* and *bequeathing* are the "practices" which are the basis for conventional procedures such as christening or making a will, which may be established in relation to them.

The importance of the linguistic dimensions of constitutional practices to the study of politics lies in their application to legal reasoning and judicial interpretation. Although the tradition of constitutional law is important to lawyers and the relation can be seen in terms of rules, even here the creative activity which advances the law stretches the characterization. At the appellate level, that creative judgment causes the most problems. Thus, it is necessary to distinguish between the rules which designate certain procedures and the grammar which reveals the practices on which the procedures are based. The impact of grammar on a decision is far more subtle and potentially more revealing than the rules that we traditionally look to for insight into the role of law in judicial interpretation.

In language, it is possible to distinguish between the grammar of some thing or activity, which tells us what the thing is, and the rules in terms of which we decide whether a particular case is a case of something which we already understand. In constitutional law, the difference may be stated in terms of statutory rules and the grammar of legal language. In regard to juries, states and the federal government designate certain groups of people to sit as juries. It is these rules which are subject to constitutional assessment.[9] In the discussion of these cases, it has been the grammar of the institution of the jury that reveals the sort of thing it is for the legal process, and it is that grammar that is basic to determining the constitutionality of the statutory rules. Justice White, in both *Williams* and *Apodaca*, went to considerable length to argue first that twelve members were not required for a jury and then that the tradition of unanimity was not essential in all cases—a ruling which observers felt stretched the tradition beyond recognition.[10] Yet, these judgments merely indicate the flexibility of constitutional grammar in a particular decision. As part of the grammar of our political life, the conceptual limits are exceedingly broad and leave much room for judicial maneuvering. Clearly, at the time of the first decision White could not have indicated that two members were required to constitute a jury. It is significant that the Court was not asked to decide that question. Rather, the very raising of the question based on statutory provisions of the states involved suggests that the constitutional grammar of the concept required some number between zero and twelve. That this may not always be the case is, of course, a matter of some concern.[11] What is possible under the Constitution is in a constant state of flux.

Law sets up procedures under the authority of the state. The initial meaning of such procedures depends on practices already understood. Legislators and judges dictate rules which, for example, relate to the proper preparation of a will, i.e., the requirements for a legal bequest. Law also establishes the grounds for perjury in order to establish the sanction to be applied to lying under oath. In many cases, it is difficult to distinguish between rules and more basic legal practices. This is often because of the special role of law and legal institutions in our social life. It is less obvious that grammatical considerations which reveal legal practices underlie the intelligibility of legal discourse. These considerations are fundamental to the meaningful use of rules and procedures whether they be in an appellate brief or a judicial opinion. The indefiniteness of some cases notwithstanding, certain practices exist which are peculiar to the legal sphere and which assume a particular role in our lives as a result of the relations established in law. Marriage, for instance, as a practice under law, is a different practice from cohabitation. It is not merely a conventional procedure stipulated for cohabitation, but something which has a different role in our lives, a state of affairs about which we can say different things than we can about cohabitation.

One of the keys to distinguishing between conventional procedures that are constituted by their rules and the practices that underlie such procedures is whether or not a specific activity can be described entirely by the rules applicable to it without reference to some fundamental practice. Procedures not founded on prior practice will be describable entirely in terms of their rules. Procedures founded on prior practice must be described both in terms of their rules and by reference to the practices in which they are rooted. In the latter cases, the activity in question has a sense as a practice, independent of the particular rules for how it is performed. Finally, if some activity is itself a practice rather than merely a conventional procedure, there must exist a way of stating, without alluding to specific rules, what the activity is or what acting in accordance with the rules amounts to.

In the constitutional tradition, a practice is defined by its grammar rather than by the rules which apply to it. Although practice will be describable entirely in terms of their rules. Procedures sense of what these practices are. The communication of this sense, i.e., what it would be relevant to say and do with regard to such a practice, is the function of grammar. Chess and making a will have often been considered in this context. We can learn what playing chess or making a will is from the rules only if we are already familiar with what kind of activity playing a game or bequeathing is. The system of rules that respectively constitute chess and the practice of making a will, for example, depends on the fact that it is possible to understand (without reference to any of the rules) what sort of thing it is that results from acting in accordance with the rules. Thus, from the requirements for making a will we can learn what a valid will is only if we already know what bequeathing is. Making a will is conventional procedure established on the basis of a practice. In this case, the specific procedures are legal.

The difference between the practices in the Constitution and related concepts in ordinary English is not always obvious. Constitutional practices are designated by English words. They look like English. Yet, many practices which have become institutionalized in constitutional law are very different from related activities not so institutionalized. "Due process" is a constitutional concept that can stand apart from ordinary interpretations of what the words mean. Indeed, in this case, the ordinary words give very little indication of constitutional meaning or significance. The constitutional concept of "due process" is different enough so that the language which is appropriate to describe it includes a significant conceptual overlay that gives it a unique meaning. The meaning here is not simply that which might have been meant by the authors of the Fourteenth Amendment, but includes the wealth of material on the meaning of the concept that has developed in the subsequent 100 years of interpretation and use of the concept. Constitutional "due process" is in this sense a practice apart from the ordinary English words that comprise it.

Constitutional law contains unique practices which suggest the validity of considering it as a language. Many of the practices that distinguish constitutional law from human activity in general derive from the legal sphere, as did so many of the words considered in Chapter 2. The fundamental aspects of constitutional law are legal; in addition, we learn a number of other more political practices when we learn the nature of the Constitution.

THE CONSTITUTION AS A LANGUAGE

Theories of language based on verification principles, like the theories of the early Wittgenstein, argue either that propositions can be ill-formed and thus violate logical rules of the language, or that they can be shown to be false by appeal to the world. The theories of language considered here emphasize that an important factor in language is the grammar of that language, i.e., what it makes sense to say. Grammar, as the foundation for the appropriate use of words, determines sense in language. The notion of sense or intelligibility has a bearing on the use of concepts in ways established by the grammar of a language. When use is inappropriate to the grammar of a language, the nature of the inappropriateness may be something other than that such use can be shown to be empirically false or illogical.

In working out the limits of the sensible, the source of an analysis is the conventions by means of which we think and talk. Waismann discusses intelligibility in grammar in terms of the conventions that prevent us from being able to make sense out of the phrase "red is industrious."[12] He argues that grammatical conventions have taught us that color words such as "red" are not the sorts of things that can be "industrious." With some effort, one could develop a context in which meaning might be accorded to this utterance. Such a context would not, however, by what we conventionally understand by the word "red."

Since constitutional law is a language because it has a unique grammar, certain statements do not make sense in the context of constitutional law. This view of constitutional law as language suggests the "legal" constraints on judicial interpretation. Some things come to be understood as appropriate to say when the language of constitutional law is learned. The determination of what is appropriate in this sense need rely neither on logic nor on an appeal to the world. What is appropriate is to a great extent a function of the grammar of constitutional law.

The appellate interpretation of the meaning of "equality," or what can properly be considered to fall within the scope of that concept, demonstrates that the grammar which shows the role of the concept in language is fundamental to raising an intelligible claim as well as to making a judgment. This is true even though such judgments may significantly alter the rules which determine the applicability of the concept in particular cases.

In laying the foundation for separate but equal in *Plessy v.*

Ferguson,[13] the Court heard the issue of whether separate facilities could still be judged equal. In deciding that there was nothing in the concept of equality, as derived from the Fourteenth Amendment, that prohibited the possibility of separate facilities being equal, the Court set a pattern of argumentation. This pattern has continued as the basis of equal protection claims. In *Mitchell v. United States* (1941),[14] the first equal protection case subsequent to 1873 which was favorable to blacks, the conceptualization evident in the *Plessy* decision continued to govern the decision-making process. The favorable decision in *Mitchell* was a result of a particular case in which the facilities were deemed not to be "substantially equal."[15] The pattern of the cases through *Mitchell* and *Brown*[16] has remained within the conceptual structure first enunciated in the *Plessy* decision.

In this regard, it would have been "false," prior to the decision in *Brown v. Board of Education* (1954), to say that constitutional law prohibited racially segregated educational facilities *per se*. To the extent that the claim was "intelligible" in 1954, it depended on a reconstruction of the conceptual possibilities in the idea of equality. A new sense was imparted by the Warren Court in its treatment of this issue by the introduction of the psychological evidence presented by the NAACP. It was the intelligibility of the claim imported from ordinary use—that the Constitution prohibited racially segregated educational facilities in spite of particular outcomes to the contrary—which made such an appeal to the Constitution reasonable. Knowledge of the concept and the room to maneuver were fundamental to raising an intelligible claim in this context. Following the holding in *Brown*, it became not only intelligible but also "true" to say that constitutional law prohibits racially segregated educational facilities.

In considering the charge that the *Brown* decision was a sociological and not a legal one, Pritchett agrees that it could not be "legal" because the precedents were against it. He argues that "the Supreme Court is not solely a Court of Law. It is a Court of Law and Justice."[17] It seems possible, however, that if the legal considerations are viewed in terms of the arguments presented, these arguments may be said to follow an established pattern. Although both sides of the argument are presented, the fact that the appeals are made with regard to what makes sense shows the importance of a tradition indicating limits to the meaningful use of a concept. It is in this regard that the "grammar" of constitutional language indicates the role of "law" in constitutional interpretation. The linguistic dimensions of law influence the decision-making of judges.

The first use of sociological evidence in constitutional adjudication is a useful case supporting this point. It has been said that Brandeis prepared his famous brief in order to meet a challenge presented in Justice Peckham's *Lochner* opinion[18] where it had been argued that there was no way to demonstrate that workers were better off with wage and hour laws.[19] Precisely because the Brandeis brief was formulated in terms of an established context and attempted to forward a line of argument, it demonstrates the influence of the "grammar" of constitutional language. While the outcome of a case is crucial to an understanding of the political factors which may have a bearing on a judicial decision, it is of relatively little importance to an understanding of the function of language in an interpretive decision.

More recent developments in this area reveal another aspect of constitutional practice that suggests the limits as well as conceptual possibilities imposed by constitutional interpretation. One of the overriding considerations has been that the Fourteenth Amendment, from which most of the decisions on equality are derived, applied to state action and not to the action of private individuals. This creates a channel within which the judges may maneuver. The Warren Court was able to "stretch" it rather grandly. The Burger Court has allowed it to move back in the other direction. Where Justice Douglas had suggested in *Garner v. Louisiana* (1961)[20] that the licensing of a restaurant might make it a public facility, in *Moose Lodge No. 107 v. Irvis* (1972),[21] Justice Rehnquist held that licensing did not sufficiently implicate the state in the discriminatory policies of the lodge. Still, equal protection means nothing in terms of the American Constitution without reference to the notion of state action. The oscillation has been around the line that draws the distinction.

Practices which exemplify the qualities just discussed are evident in both the procedural requirements by which constitutional law operates and the structural arrangements and guarantees that make up the constitutional system and the Bill of Rights. The legal practices which make constitutional interpretation what it is determine how constitutional claims are raised, i.e., the appropriate manner of invoking the Constitution. The substantive considerations are those legal practices that may be the basis of a particular appeal. Judicial interpretation of claims brought on the basis of these practices depends on knowledge of what the practices are, i.e., how they fit into the constitutional framework. Both considerations suggest the legal foundations of constitutional law, which are part of the grammar of constitutional language.

One of the procedural considerations which come from the law is fundamental to legal discourse generally, as well as to the Constitution. It is the requirement of a case or controversy. A controversy has generally been interpreted as something on the order of a real dispute between the plaintiff and the defendant. Indeed, the concepts plaintiff and defendant depend on the idea of a dispute. The grammar of judicial activity reveals that what the courts do is settle claims. Although borderline cases are immensely important for understanding the substance of constitutional law, it can be said that for the most part constitutional adjudication does not "speak to" anything but cases or controversies. Thus, this practice is fundamental to constitutional law.

In determining what sorts of things are subject to constitutional adjudication, the "case or controversy" requirement indicated one aspect of the language of constitutional law. Wittgenstein proposes that "to imagine a language means to imagine a form of life."[22] To imagine constitutional law as a language, it is appropriate to consider the usage which is the source of the constitutional form of life. The case or controversy requirement gives some indication of the nature of this form of life and one of the essential ways in which constitutional adjudication differs from other political activity.

Other considerations emerge from the nature of the appellate process and the position of the Supreme Court in the national judicial system as the highest court of appeal. The practices which tell us what an appeal to the Constitution entails determine when and on what basis constitutional claims are appropriate. A claim for violation of due process, for instance, presupposes some governmental action on the basis of which the claim can be made. The appellate process, being a "review" process, presupposes that a case has proceeded to a certain point before it is "ripe" for review. It would not make *sense* to ask an appellate court to award damages on a constitutional basis at the inception of a normal personal injury claim, although, on appeal, an award already granted is more likely to reach a final settlement. Constitutional law presupposes a body of common law on the basis of which most litigation is handled. As it bears largely on the process of review, constitutional law is a kind of second-order legal language.

The function of the Constitution in the appellate process, like the case or controversy requirement, forms an external boundary for constitutional language. Another practice bearing on the operation of constitutional law is that of "retroactivity." This consideration has been shown to be of a highly political nature because of the influence of popular feedback on the judicial decision in cases which deal with retroactivity.[23] Decisions in these cases have been shown to vary according to the nature of the crime committed and the state of public attitudes toward the original rule-making case. However, this political element in the decision-making of the Court is not inconsistent with the assertion that the concept of retroactivity depends on an understanding of judicial practice. Retroactivity is another practice which the language of constitutional law shares with law in general.

Some substantive legal considerations which are the subject of constitutional interpretation are those provided for in the Bill of Rights. The provisions relating to trials, juries, warrants, witnesses, counsel, and defense can only be understood on the basis of the legal form of life. The practices which underlie these provisions, like the words which express them (as has been noted in Chapter 2), depend on legal activity for their meaning. The fact that these legal concepts are also elements of the Constitution suggests that the concepts, as evident in the provisions of the Bill of Rights, depend for their meaning on understanding their constitutional as well as their legal role.

The interpretation of the constitutional right to trial by jury is an example of an issue rooted in both the common law and the constitution. In the case of *Williams v. Florida* (1970),[24] the issue was whether fewer than twelve persons could constitute a jury in other than capital cases. It is obvious that the Court's interpretation of this issue had to rely on some sense of what a jury is. Whatever the decision in the case, in order for a judgment to be made at all some knowledge of the grammar of "jury" was essential. In order to determine the number of people which should constitute a jury, the judge must know what a jury is. The idea of a jury depends on a unique "practice" which is only understood in terms of the language of law.

Other practices have legal dimensions, although their source is the political or ideological positions formalized in the Constitution. These practices rely on the nature of that document and the political and economic realities emerging from the constitutional structure. Like legal practices, political practices may also be broken down into those delineating the operations of the constitutional structure and those of a more substantive nature. Both types of practices exemplify the unique political foundations of constitutional language.

Judicial review is a constitutional practice of basically political origin. Since it functions in a highly political matrix, the complexity of the constitutional system tells as much about the nature of the practice as do the opinions which rely on it. It is sufficient here to recognize the uniqueness of this practice in the American constitutional system. The tradition of judicial review of the actions of the other branches tells us that the Court can impinge on the more explicitly political governing bodies to an undetermined extent.

The commerce power is another example of a practice which depends on certain relations in the Constitution. It is procedural in that it determines how congressional activities are to be measured for their appropriateness. The ordinary notion of "commerce" has been appealed to in judicial decisions delineating the scope of the power in the constitutional context.[25] As much as any provision in the Constitution, however, the commerce clause has attained its meaning from experience. Since Chief Justice Marshall's original interpretation of "commerce" in terms of "commercial intercourse,"[26] the application of the term in constitutional law has produced a very specialized meaning. There need be no actual commercial character to the "interstate movement," which soon became the most significant criterion.[27] While Webster's compilation continues to emphasize "business dealings," in its definition of commerce the constitutional concept need include neither interstate transport[28] nor commercial intercourse.[29] The Supreme Court's use of "commerce" has placed more emphasis on such dimensions as crime[30] and racial discrimination[31] to infuse the concept with its present meaning. As it delineates a concept in constitutional law, the meaning of "interstate commerce" is a product of experience.[32] The practice has been a political one because its use has been a reflection of the relationship between the nation and the states.

The guarantee against unreasonable searches and seizures can be considered as an example of a substantive provision of a political or ideological nature. The concept "unreasonable searches and seizures" is seated in the provisions of the first ten Amendments to the Constitution. The underlying sense of this provision emerges from the ideological position of the entire Bill of Rights and the relations between individuals and the government that are suggested therein. The basic notion of a guarantee and the ideological foundations of the Bill of Rights indicate the role of such a concept in the language of constitutional law. Like the substantive legal considerations, "unreasonable searches and seizures" may mean something outside of the Constitution. But the constitutional concept, in that it is based on the relations set up in the Bill of Rights, means what it does to the student of the Constitution because of the role the concept assumes in the language of constitutional law.

In the consideration of the "reasonableness" of a search, traditional practice has a bearing on interpretation. In *Olmstead v. United States* (1928),[33] a new technique for obtaining evidence, that of the tapping of telephone lines, was not considered a search in the traditional sense. The wiretap was not a search in the protected sense because no actual entrance was undertaken. As Pritchett notes, the tradition had been that there could be "no search without a trespass and no seizure without a physical object."[34]

The importance of the notion of penetration is evident in *Silverman v. United States* (1968).[35] Here, the penetration "by even a fraction of an inch" of an eavesdropping device was taken to constitute an intrusion into a protected area. The problem of the "seizure" of words remained to be settled in *Katz v. U.S.* (1967)[36] and required a new formulation based on the union of the search and seizure provision with the self-incrimination provision. However, the new conceptual formulation depended on an already established practice, that of individual protection against self-incrimination.

According to the formulation of the difference between rules and practices, new practices can be established on the basis of rules only when there already exists "relevant ways of speaking and acting, prior to the setting up of the rules."[37] New rules depend for their meaning on the sense of an activity which they are supposed to formulate. Thus, the "grammar of a behavior according to rules" is fundamental to the creation of new practices on the basis of rules.[38]

Constitutional interpretation of "unreasonable searches and seizures" may alter the rules by which the concept is to be evaluated, but interpretation presupposes knowledge of the role of the concept in the language of the Constitution. It is not the rules for reasonableness that define the activity; rather it is the grammar of an activity which makes it an activity of a given kind. The grammar of an activity is a matter of what things are relevant, appropriate, or make sense to say with regard to the activity. By the standard of language in general, constitutional law is highly creative, but any decision on the rules of a concept presupposes knowledge of the role of the activity to which the rules apply. At no point is it reasonable to go beyond what it makes sense to say with the expectation of being understood. The evolution of the language of the Constitution must necessarily be slow enough so that its sense is maintained.

INTRODUCING PRIVACY INTO THE CONSTITUTION

The development of privacy as a legal right began outside of the constitutional setting. Arguments, dissents, and ultimately majority opinions established its meaning for constitutional law. The way in which the concept developed in the constitutional setting is an example of the influence of the structure of constitutional language. The common law concept of privacy at the beginning was a conceptual step removed from the document and had a different meaning from the concept that has emerged in the Constitution. That this kind of creative development is at the periphery of sensible constitutional adjudication is evident in its uniqueness and in the controversy which it has generated. That the development of constitutional privacy is not outside the bounds of the sensible is evident not only by the fact that the step has been taken, but also by the fact that privacy continues to be addressed, if not expanded. The way in which the concept of privacy has been altered as it has been introduced into a new sphere reveals the power and coherence of that sphere.

Judge Cooley provided the seed, the still-evident phrasing, in articulating a right "to be let alone," in 1888.[39] Advocacy of this notion as a "right to privacy" by Samuel Warren and Louis Brandeis in 1890 in the *Harvard Law Review* launched the common law concept. Warren and Brandeis anticipated that "political, social, and economic" forces would support the inclusion of a new right in the common law. They concluded that "the right to liberty secures the exercise of extensive civil privileges; and the term 'property' has grown to comprise every form of possession—intangible, as well as tangible."[40] These proper Bostonians were responding to a new technology, the instantaneous photography which was then becoming available to mass circulation newspapers. The traditional limitations existing in the law of libel and slander were too narrow. Seeking a broader right "to determine the extent to which thoughts, sentiments and emotions will be communicated," Warren and Brandeis extrapolated from a number of common law protections. They saw principles protecting "personal production" like writing to be directed not toward theft but against publication, indicating that it was based not on private property but on what they called "an inviolate personality."[41] They hoped to establish the "right to be let alone." This remarkably successful law review article comes as close to being the source of a legal concept as can be found in case law.

A legal right to privacy thus emerged in the last century in America. Rooted in the ideology of liberalism and reflected in the common law, the right appeared as a protection against technological threats to private life. This articulation, in its form, content, and social base, influenced the introduction of privacy into the constitutional setting. Legal interest in privacy can be shown in early suggestions by the Supreme Court that privacy is an attribute of constitutionally protected rights. Its attention to threats beyond physical trespass and criminal prosecution, as well as its identification with protections against technology as employed in a mass society, made privacy a conceptually fruitful tool. The sort of constitutional right which it has become was, however, also a product of adjudication in that unique sphere. Although constitutional privacy owes much to the use of a similar concept in the common law, a rather different right developed in the Constitution as a result of its structure and traditions.

Louis D. Brandeis brought his interest in privacy with him to the Supreme Court. In 1928,[42] he issued a prophetic dissent that would reflect the path of the Supreme Court's development of the privacy concept for the next forty years and would emerge in an opinion of the court[43] two years after the "right of privacy" was authoritatively established. The 1928 case dealt with telephone wiretaps which the majority on the Court did not believe violated the protections against searches and seizures. For Brandeis, the taps were evidence of the "subtler and more far-reaching means of invading privacy that have become available to the government." Over and against these means, Brandeis argued that "the makers of our Constitution conferred, as against the government, the right to be let alone—the most comprehensive of rights and the right most valued by civilized men."[44] His opinion was a reaffirmation of his law review statement of forty years before, and it relied for constitutional application on an 1886 decision that "the Fourth and Fifth Amendments run almost into each other."[45] Joining the protections against warrantless searches and self-incrimination was to be fundamental to the development of the concept of privacy in the Constitution.

In 1942, Justice Murphy took the concept a step further. He cited the 1890 law review article and indicated that "one of the great boons secured to the inhabitants of this country by the Bill of Rights is the right of personal privacy guaranteed by the Fourth

Amendment.''[46] The opinion indicated growing concern over searches and seizures. It is thus linked with the early conception of privacy. Justice Frankfurter further embedded privacy in the constitutional protections of liberty seven years later when he indicated that ''security of one's privacy against arbitrary intrusion by the police—which is at the core of the Fourth Amendment—is basic to a free society. It is therefore implicit in the 'concept of ordered liberty.' ''[47] Here, the explicit reliance on privacy as a key to the decision, and its inclusion among things fundamental, added another tier of support for the emerging right.

As he maintained his close ties to the legacy of Brandeis, Justice Douglas's interest in a private sphere extended the concept beyond the limits suggested by his predecessor. In 1951, a lower court had held radio programs on federally supervised buses to be in violation both of the Fifth Amendment in that they constituted ''forced listening'' and of the First Amendment in that they encroached on ''freedom of attention.''[48] The Supreme Court, however, treated the claim as an invasion of privacy, a possible ground given other developments, but not the one explicitly and painstakingly developed by the Court of Appeals. The majority opinion by Justice Burton rang with denials that the right of privacy applied in this case. It is unclear, however, where in the case history he got the notion to which he directed his opinion. One possibility is, of course, Justice Douglas, whose dissent concerned the right dismissed by the Court:

The case comes down to the meaning of ''liberty'' as used in the Fifth Amendment. Liberty in the constitutional sense must mean more than freedom from unlawful governmental restraint; it must include privacy as well, if it is to be a repository of freedom. The right to be let alone is indeed the beginning of all freedom.[49]

Privacy had thus become a recognized constitutional practice before it received the authoritative sanction from a majority of the Supreme Court. In addition to these cases which discussed the right to privacy, it had been argued extensively before the legal profession[50] and had an impact on the feasibility of litigation in pursuit of emerging claims. The acceptance of the right by a majority of the

Court is, however, the ultimate sanction placed on the intelligibility of the concept. Privacy may have made "constitutional sense" before the Justices authorized its use, but it was never so evident as when it received the sanction that made it law.

Griswold v. Connecticut (1965)[51] is the benchmark in recognition of the constitutional right of privacy. Even in this case, however, the opinion written by Douglas made a more limited claim than the dissents, law review commentary, and some subsequent decisions have chosen to recognize. Although Douglas referred to "penumbras, formed by emanations" from the First, Third, Fourth, Fifth, and Ninth Amendments,[52] he held the Connecticut contraceptive use statute unconstitutional because enforcement would require prying into the privacy of the home. The ground was the more limited right to marital privacy, "a right of privacy older than the Bill of Rights."[53]

Justice Black dissented from the opinion of the Court because he desired the holding to be based on "some specific constitutional provision." He paid homage to Warren's and Brandeis's collaborative effort, but objected to the exaltation of a phrase "used in discussing grounds for tort relief, to the level of a constitutional rule." Black's view was consistent with his general concern for more literal interpretation. His contribution was his description of privacy as a general constitutional right. It was a stand which Douglas, even in supporting the expansion of the concept, was careful to avoid. Black was not advancing the right in the same way as had been the case in prior dissents. It was in reaction to the holding that he acknowledged a stronger role for the concept than that put forward by the majority opinion.

This tendency continued in other forums following the decision. Legal commentary subsequent to *Griswold* directed its attention to the new right.[54] Whether arguing for or against it, "the right of privacy" had become a point of contention. In this literature, Emerson's discussion indicates the variety of choices open to the judges. Of the variety of claims put forth, Emerson contends that the important thing is that "six Justices found such a right [to privacy] to exist, and thereby established it for the first time as an independent constitutional right."[55] He had argued the case and thus must be considered responsibile for the sensible perception that the Supreme Court was ready to acknowledge a right grounded in freedom of speech and protection from unconstitutional criminal prosecution rather than the common law protections of private property and reputation. (Further discussion of the use of the constitutional concept of privacy by the Supreme Court is presented in Chapter 8.)

Constitutional law, at least for the Supreme Court, is more like a primary natural language than like a second or technical language. In learning a second language, for the most part we learn words for practices which we already know. In constitutional law, as is evident in the case of privacy, the word is the same but its use and the practice it designates are different. Although, in tracing its history, the role of the common law concept is important, the use of constitutional privacy is in important respects at odds with the use to be made of the root concept. If constitutional law merely consisted of new words or even special rules for already existing practices, then the description of law as language would tell us very little about the unique linguistic considerations bearing on judicial behavior. However, unique practices of procedural and substantive significance for interpretation underlie the language of the Constitution and suggest that it can be considered to have a grammar of its own. This is the key to the importance of considering the decision-making process in constitutional law from a linguistic perspective.

NOTES

1. Philbrick, op. cit.; Mellinkoff, op. cit.

2. Cavell, *Must We Mean What We Say?*, pp. 19–20.

3. Hubert Schwyzer, "Concepts," p. 112.

4. Ibid., pp. 105–106.

5. Ibid., p. 106. See also John Searle, "How to Derive 'Ought' from 'Is'." In *Theories of Ethics,* ed. Philippa Foot (New York: Oxford University Press, 1967); John Rawls, op. cit.

6. Schwyzer, "Concepts," p. 161.

7. J. L. Austin, *How to Do Things with Words* (New York: Oxford University Press, 1965).

8. Schwyzer, "Concepts," p. 161.

9. *Apodaca v. Oregon*, 406 U.S. 404 (1972); *Williams v. Florida*, 399 U.S. 78 (1970).

10. Ibid.; Pritchett, *American Constitution*, p. 467.

11. Hans Zeisel, " . . . And Then There Were None: The Diminution of the Federal Jury," *University of Chicago Law Review* 38 (1971):710.

12. Waismann, op. cit., p. 37.

13. 163 U.S. 537 (1896).

14. 313 U.S. 80.

15. Pritchett, *Civil Liberties*, p. 127.

16. 347 U.S. 483 (1954), 349 U.S. 204 (1955).

17. Pritchett, *The Political Offender and the Warren Court* (Boston: Boston University Press, 1958), p. 62.

18. *Lochner v. New York*, 198 U.S. 45 (1905).

19. Samuel Krislov, *The Supreme Court in the Political Process* (New York: Macmillan Co., 1965), p. 72.

20. 368 U.S. 157 (1961).

21. 407 U.S. 163 (1972).

22. Wittgenstein, *Philosophical Investigations*, par. 19.

23. G. Gregory Fahlund, "Retroactivity and the Warren Court," *Journal of Politics* 34 (1973):592.

24. Op. cit.

25. *Gibbons v. Ogden*, 9 Wheat. 1 (1824).

26. Ibid.

27. *Covington Bridge Co. v. Kentucky*, 154 U.S. 204 (1894).

28. *U.S. v. Darby Lumber Co.*, 312 U.S. 100 (1941).

29. *Caminetti v. U.S.*, 242 U.S. 470 (1917).

30. *U.S. v. Bass*, 404 U.S. 336 (1971).

31. *Katzenbach v. McClung,* 379 U.S. 294 (1964).

32. Pritchett, *American Constitution*, p. 180.

33. 277 U.S. 438.

34. Pritchett, *American Constitution*, p. 163.

35. 365 U.S. 505.

36. 389 U.S. 347.

37. Schwyzer, "Concepts," p. 122.

38. Ibid.

39. Thomas M. Cooley, *Treatise on Torts,* 2nd ed. (Chicago: Callaghan and Co., 1888).

40. Samuel D. Warren and Louis Brandeis, "The Right to Privacy," *Harvard Law Review* 4 (1890):193.

41. Ibid., p. 141.

42. *Olmstead v. U.S.*, 277 U.S. 438 (1928).

43. *Katz v. U.S.*, 389 U.S. 347 (1967).

44. *Olmstead v. U.S.*, 473.

45. *Boyd v. U.S.*, 116 U.S. 616 (1886).

46. *Goldman v. U.S.*, 316 U.S. 129 (1942), 136.

47. *Wolf v. Colorado*, 338 U.S. 25 (1949).

48. *Pollak v. Public Utilities Commission*, 191 F. 2nd 450 (1951).

49. *PUC v. Pollak*, 343 U.S. 451 (1951), 467.

50. William M. Beaney, "The Constitutional Right to Privacy," *Supreme Court Review* 212 (1962):212–251; Erwin N. Griswold, "The Right to Be Let Alone," *Northwestern University Law Review* 55 (1960): 216.

51. 381 U.S. 479 (1965).

52. Ibid., 484.

53. Ibid., 486.

54. Robert G. Dixon, *The Right of Privacy* (New York: DaCapo Press, 1971).

55. Chaim Perelman, op. cit.; Stephen Toulmin, *Uses of Argument;* Dixon, op. cit.

7 | The Use of Language and Judicial Interpretation

The aspect of language examined here is the language user's ability to make an infinite number of new sentences from the grammatical patterns previously described as fundamental to language use. An association is proposed between a decision as to how to "go on" in a new situation with language and the decision of the Supreme Court as to what it is appropriate to say about a particular constitutional issue. Judicial decision is described as a linguistic act. That is, on the Supreme Court when a Justice confronts a new issue, as whether the provision for a jury is satisfied by a body of six persons, the process of decision is analogous to the ordinary situation when an individual is presented with an opportunity to say something that he or she has never said before. The intent here is to suggest the utility of language analysis for understanding the nature of legal politics by demonstrating the similarities between linguistic interpretation and interpretation of the Constitution by the Supreme Court.

LINGUISTIC PRACTICE AND THE NATURE OF INTERPRETATION

The decision of a Justice, when interpreting a constitutional provision, parallels the situation in ordinary language when the speaker decides how to formulate an appropriate sentence in a novel context. Traditionally, theories of language have implied that rules exist by which language can be judged. Modern linguistic theory explains the use of language, especially the stringing together of words, by reference to the capacity of the speaker to make intelligible statements. Explanation of this process of interpretation has distinguished modern theories from the empiricist theory of language. Attention to this issue makes modern conceptions of ordinary language important for depicting what the Justices go through when they analyze a case.

The language of law is not purely legal; it emerges from ordinary discourse.[1] Ordinary language is essential for discussion of legal concepts. It has an on-going significance in their development. The special quality of legal language lies not in its terms but rather in the development of particular legal practices. Learning the language of constitutional law entails grasping the nature of these practices. In establishing a correlation between language and law, the aspects of judicial decision are demonstrable without dependence on the conception of formal rule-following in terms of precedent. This thesis suggests that what distinguishes judicial interpretation from other kinds of political activity is a particular linguistic capacity.

In "going on in the same way" in novel situations, language presents certain guides for the appropriate decisions, but only as a result of practice, not because of a set of rules. It is more accurate to describe judicial decision on the Supreme Court as consisting of making judgments as a result of practice rather than in accordance with a rule. In ordinary language, the speaker's choice as to how to "go on" must conform to appropriate practice. Following the guidelines of the linguistic model, questions of "going on" in a language can be settled only by reference to convention. No logical necessity or empirical referent is governing.[2]

In his *Philosophical Investigations*, Wittgenstein describes some dimensions of "going on" as he understands them. Knowing the principles that allow one to proceed intelligibly does not mean that some formula has occurred to the speaker. At least, when we are able to use language we cannot usually say that the capacity is one to be explained as the revelation of some formula. No such occurrence can be described as happening behind or side by side with the act of "going on." When we traditionally think of the operation of precedent in the law, it is more like such a formula than like the linguistic or conceptual competence that more accurately describes the basis of a Justice's ability to see a new situation that fits into the patterns and trends of the law. According to the description of language,

> If there has to be anything "behind the utterances of the formula" it is *particular circumstances*, which justify me in saying I can go on—when the formula occurs to me.
> Try not to think of understanding as a "mental process" at all. —For *that* is the expression which confuses you. But ask yourself: in what sort of case, in what kind of circumstances, do we say, "Now I know how to go on," when that is, the formula has occurred to me?—[3]

According to this view, no single prescriptive rule or formula serves as a guide, but rather the whole body of experience through which we have learned how to use the language. Wittgenstein points out that there is nothing behind our ability to proceed that is more certain than this body of experience. He cautions against thinking of formulating sentences as a mental process because such a conception suggests a calculation on the basis of prescriptive rules. He proposes that we emphasize *when* it is appropriate to go on in a certain way rather than *why*.

When Justice Blackmun used the concept of privacy in the 1973 abortion decision, he explained that the Court has recognized the right and that it was "broad enough to encompass a woman's decision whether or not to terminate her pregnancy."[4] According to the discussion of "going on," we can say of Blackmun's decision that the circumstances which reveal the use of the privacy concept provided him with a conceptual capacity. By those circumstances, he could view state regulation of abortion as at least a potential intrusion on the right. The situation is, of course, different from ordinary speech, given the assistance afforded the Justice by such things as lawyers' briefs and oral argument. Yet, we can still say that the circumstances of prior use (which are employed in the opinion as justifications) rather than a formula or mental picture enable the Justice to decide.

In these investigations, Wittgenstein attacks a view of linguistic activity which suggests that in our imagination we perform an operation which is like fitting something to a definite shape.[5] Such a view perpetuates the idea of an "essence" of meaning, since it suggests that the activity of "going on" is like doing a second thing that is identical with the first. Wittgenstein proposes, on the other hand, that "going on in the same way" must be appropriate to the body of convention that surrounds the activity: ". . . when he suddenly knew how to go on, when he understood the principle, . . . it is *the* circumstances under which he had such an experience that justify him in saying in such a case that he understands, that he knows how to go on."[6] The body of conventions in operation are proposed as a description of going on rather than the traditional reliance on mental processes which is inconsistent with the use theory of meaning.

The following passages demonstrate what it would mean, for Wittgenstein, that a particular usage "fits" in this sense of being appropriate:

It would be quite misleading . . . to call the words a "description of a mental state." —One might rather call them "signal;" and we judge whether it was rightly employed by what he goes on to do.[7]

A person goes by a sign-post only in so far as there exists a regular use of sign-posts, a custom.[8]

To obey a rule, to make a report, to give an order, to play a game of chess, are customs (uses, institutions).[9]

The grammar which explains these activities is not a prescriptive set of rules but rather a way of indicating or describing the character of the experience which stands as a guide to linguistic use. The speaker of a language may be hard pressed to identify a particular rule which is the basis for his decision to say something in one way rather than another. It is not rule-following that enables a native speaker to use language but rather the body of conventions.

In the case of privacy in the Constitution, like other instances of judicial decision by Justices of the Supreme Court, past experience is closer to custom than to the idea of a rule. Regular use or even, as in this case, simply some instance of accepted use provides the conceptual possibility for symbolic action. It does not compel. In the case of privacy, Blackmun had the opportunity to use or not to use the concept in the particular case. He did not have the opportunity to use privacy in unintelligible ways or to introduce some new concept picked up in foreign travels. Knowledge of constitutional law affects the initial judgment as to whether a claim is worth hearing. It sets the parameters for the decision and provides a basis for elaborating an opinion. In law, as in ordinary language, events can only be understood if they relate to some body of symbolic communication. Prior knowledge indicates how they are to be interpreted.

In the context of behavioral research, to assert that a limited body of claims is intelligible raises compelling questions about the impact of tradition on judicial action. Legal battles are fought at a margin of clarity which presumes an understanding of constitutional language. With regard to "state action," for instance, Justices have at times "stretched" the concept in order to make a claim, but the requirement does operate as a conceptual constraint and hence as a limit to action. The concept can "be used as the basis for not extending rights, more easily than it can be used to further those rights."[10] Such constraints operate not because they are rules but because they are conventions supplying meaning through use.

Barry Stroud, a philosopher working in the Wittgensteinian tradition, offers a description of "going on" in language that conveys the effect of grammar. He argues that the sense of appropriate utterances that operates is not "like rails that stretch to infinity and compel us to go on in one and only one way."[11] But neither is it the case that there is no compulsion. The guides, the indication of what it is appropriate to do, are those of experience.

. . . there are the rails we have already travelled, and we can extend them beyond the present point only by depending on those that already exist. In order for the rails to be navigible they must be extended in smooth and natural ways; how they are to be continued is to that extent determined by the route of those rails which are already there.[12]

This vivid metaphor is immediately applicable to the Supreme Court. It has the continuity that is evident in judicial decision without losing the creative, human dimension. It calls attention not to moving down the track, but to laying down the tracks. This is the very nature of how constitutional formulations emerge and of the development of new concepts by incorporation into a particular setting.

This conception of what it is to "go on" from one series of cases to another in a new context is substantiated by Hunter's interpretation of the use theory of meaning. Hunter believes that the substitution of "use" for "meaning" weighs against the unprofitable pursuit of the "essence" of meaning. The conception of "essential" qualities as a basis for the use of language has traditionally led to the belief that skill in language results from knowledge of a procedure. Hunter views the training essential to language as "a sort of tuning the human organism until it simply performs well linguistically."[13] In a related fashion, Wittgenstein characterizes the understanding of language as the mastery of a technique.[14] According to Wittgenstein's conception of language learning, in learning language the child must master how the words of its language are used. The clues to such skill, as stated earlier, are contained in the examples which show how words are used.[15]

Knowledge of language is dynamic because it emerges from the circumstances of use. Such knowledge is distinct from the knowledge of a state of affairs.[16] A person who knows a language "knows how" to use words, concepts, and structures often without "knowing that" such use is correct for certain reasons. "Knowing how" entails the ability to project what has been learned in one situation into new situations.

The conventional structures of language determine how these projections are to be made, and these structures have a social foundation. When Peter Winch applied Wittgenstein's theories to the social sciences, he emphasized the importance of rules in characterizing human activity that is symbolic.[17] Because law is generally associated with a very different set of rules, this aspect of Winch's important treatment has not been employed. Rather, the emphasis has been on the notion of grammar as previously discussed and on "practices." These considerations are contextual rather than formal, and Winch supports this characteristic. Rather than being "outside" and operating on the actor, practices describe human activity. Thus, for Winch, "the whole substance of Wittgenstein's argument is that it is not those practices considered on their own which justify the application of categories like language and meaning, but the social context in which these practices are found."[18] This point has been amplified by Stanley Cavell, who assures us that neither the assimilation of a book of rules nor the awareness of universal properties will guarantee that the proper projections will take place. As he has said, "That . . . we do go on is a matter of our sharing routes of interest and feeling, modes of response . . . all the whirl of organism Wittgenstein calls 'forms of life.'"[19] Language operates in a fashion distinct from logic. "Shared modes of response," rather than an ideal formulation, suggest how we are to go on.

The importance of these modes for describing how grammar functions in the process of "going on" makes this perspective on language appropriate in examining how legal activity, particularly constitutional interpretation at the appellate level, differs from other forms of political activity. In the language of constitutional law, as in language generally, the familiarity with a way of proceeding—agreement in certain conventions—is the basis for linguistic projections.

The capacity to proceed in the linguistic sense just described is evident in the unique judicial responsibility for deciding both what to decide and how to decide. In the decision as to what cases to look at carefully, the Supreme Court sifts through over 4,000 claims. For the most part, these claims have already been filtered by lawyers in accordance with previous indications of judicial interest. Yet, as Justice Douglas has said, the claims "are often fantastic, surpassing credulity."[20] When a Justice finds a claim credible, that decision is a necessary condition for its being accepted. If it does not fit into the framework of constitutional language, that is, if the Justice cannot see the instance being described as a case of even a potentially valid constitutional claim, the claim, of course, has no chance of success.

In the case of *Gideon v. Wainwright* (1963),[21] for instance, the Justices found Gideon's claim for representation by a lawyer to be one of potential merit. Although the claim he made, that he was constitutionally guaranteed a lawyer, was not technically true when he made it, it may be said to have made sense to the Justices. On a subsequent conviction (with representation) for the same offense, however, Gideon's claim that his second trial violated the double jeopardy provisions of the Constitution did not make any sense and was not reviewed by the Court.

LEGAL TRAINING AND LINGUISTIC PRACTICE

Law has shared concerns that generate its particular vocabulary, conventional modes of response that give it some predictability, and a unique "form of life" that distinguishes it from other types of activity. These characteristics were described in the previous chapter as the basis upon which constitutional law could be considered a language. For Julius Stone, "Lawyer-language is more practiced than talked about, and easier recognized than described, yet familiar from training and daily experience to all practitioners and to jurists who handle the products of practice."[22] It is appropriate at this point to consider the learning process which ultimately determines the use of legal language.

Knowledge of constitutional language involves an ability which influences the activity of lawyers and judges. Where attitudes and social background are used alone to measure the judicial decision, legal interpretation is placed in conflict with political factors; the result is that one or another factor is taken to characterize the process. When the linguistic model is used, whether or not political considerations have a bearing on the decision does not detract from the fact that judges possess a skill which is fundamental to interpretive behavior.

Legal training imparts the tradition and conceptual foundations on which the legal process operates. Modern linguistic theory provides a way of assessing the impact of this training on the behavior of judges by proposing a less rigid measure of law than the traditional reliance on precedent and *stare decisis*. The uniqueness of legal language sets those who know how to use it, and whose activity provides a forum for such use, apart from other political actors. Many who are not lawyers or judges know something of the legal language, and many with legal training do not practice only as attorneys. Knowing the language of law can be a useful tool in a variety of endeavors because it involves an expertise of social significance.

Walter Probert argues that legal terms acquire a "factual, descriptive sort of base."[23] Lawyers cannot just use words in any way they wish, but rather "the definition(s) must be tenable/acceptable. As times and conditions change, what is acceptable or potentially persuasive varies. Even then, one has to know his audience."[24] Thus, the language of the law both facilitates political action and limits it. It is perhaps this paradoxical quality of language that makes it so difficult to examine in political terms. Yet, with law, it is the conceptual structure which, along with the individual capacities of attorneys, is the power of the law. When a lawyer determines that a particular event does indeed constitute something legally governed, the translation of an accident into a liability action or a prejudicial act into a constitutional violation becomes possible. The symbolic structure of the law, for lawyers as well as for Supreme Court Justices, will enable some things to be handled and will preclude legal treatment of some others. Like any tool, legal concepts make things possible, but because the legal community is absolutely dependent on them, some things that might once have been possible may no longer be so because of a new orientation.

Similar capacities result from training in constitutional law. For example, knowledge of the traditional application of the law of search and seizure (at the time of the *Olmstead* case) to the penetration of a private residence and the seizure of physical objects becomes a sort of conceptual resistance to any other interpretation of the law. Conversely, knowledge of the law of self-incrimination provisions enabled the use, in the *Katz* decision, of a combination of the Fourth and Fifth Amendments. Familiar concepts, applied in novel ways, suggest the potential of concepts to facilitate new modes of response.

At the same time that a tool enables events to be conceived in certain ways, it also places limitations on other possible conceptions. There is no denying that legal syntax is the basis of creative argument—that the work of legal scholars to fashion new conceptual tools has not advanced their perception of society's interests. But the aspect of law most relevant to the characterization of the legal dimension in the judicial decision is that which functions as a limitation. It has thus been said of legal language that "it is usually offered to inhibit the thought process of the audience."[25] Indeed, its very uniqueness cannot help but obscure the many other ways in which a situation might be seen and thus prevent other possibilities for political action. Both the limiting and the liberating effect of established conceptualizations are part of the impact of language on interpretation in constitutional law, as experience with any number of concepts from state action to privacy indicates.

In his discussion of legal reasoning, Julius Stone supports the relation between linguistic knowledge, conceptual training, and the judicial decision. He describes the achievements of precedent law to be "a function, not just of the theory, but of the largely unarticulated techniques of operating it."[26] These techniques and ideals are the substantive basis of the contention that legal activity is analogous to the activity of using language. Not simply the acquisition of a respect for the past, or norms of conduct, but the learned ways in which events are to be seen—if they are to be dealt with in constitutional terms—govern the decision at the highest appellate level.

In his introduction to *Renner's Institutions of Private Law and Their Social Function*,[27] O. Kahn-Freund offers another view on the development of legal institutions. He proposes that the processes of the common law should be understood as the outcome of the specific requirements and the tradition of the guild organization of the legal profession. The result, he argues, was that English law "evolved as a series of guild rules for the use and guidance of the members and apprentices of the Inns of Court."[28] In this sense, the common law has its roots in the practices of a craft that led to more technical rules which would instruct the lawyer in how to go about the activity of raising and defending claims.

The importance of technical training and background in legal activity is also developed by Alf Ross, for whom the techniques of law determine the nature of the process. According to Ross, the activity of "weighing and formulating" which is basic to the activity of judging is "not based on theoretical insight" (notwithstanding the claims of law schools which profess simply to be

honing young minds for the advice and judgment that they claim
are required of the lawyer). Rather, the activity is based on "a
skill which must be developed by training."[29] This training is the
acquaintance with the legal tradition that makes up the bulk of the
law school curriculum. To be able to practice, an aspiring student
of law must not simply become wise, but he or she must learn a new
language. According to Probert, "a law student acquires legal
valuations by learning to talk law."[30] Once the knowledge of a
language is acquired, it affects how the students see the world.
Every Justice of the Supreme Court has been such a student at one
time. Although some judicial behavioralists have relied on precedent as a measure of legal activity, it is an inadequate measure
since it minimizes the technical skill and linguistic capacities which
enable the Justice to make sense out of what is presented to him.
Precedents do not adequately describe what law is any more than
definitions of words and traditional grammar describe language.

The linguistic model of "going on," as applied to legal interpretation, proposes a description of judicial creativity that is not
necessarily outside of "the law." The linguistic dimension in the
judicial decision portrays new substantive developments in law as
sharing the qualities of action in accordance with established
patterns. In law, the relation of general concepts to particular
cases (like the use of language which is both novel and appropriate)
is creative to a certain extent.

The stress on interaction and dialectical learning that has come to
characterize learning in law by means of the case method is an
attempt to begin the process of legal training in a fashion which is
consistent with the growth of legal competence through practice.[31]
Initial legal training and legal practice may be seen in terms of the
kind of learning process which ordinary language philosophers
have made one of the essential elements of their criticism of the
empiricist theory of language.

In learning law, the law student begins to put together the new
conceptions that will enable him to continue the learning process
himself. Again, the similarity to Wittgenstein's conception of
language learning is evident:

When the boy or grown-up learns what one might call special technical language, e.g., the use of charts and diagrams, descriptive geometry, chemical symbolism, etc., he learns more language games.

(Remark: The picture we have of the language of the grown-up is that of a nebulous mass of language, his mother tongue, surrounded by discrete and more or less clear-cut language games, the technical language.)[32]

Ordinarily, we continue to add to our language, and this we do through the basic linguistic capacities that we have acquired. In a substantially new language, like law, the learning process starts when the student or young practitioner first begins to understand the role of unique practices; their particular applications continue to be worked out in use.

The similarity between law and language has been used to relate ordinary language philosophy to the study of politics. Hannah Pitkin uses the common law to demonstrate the use theory of meaning discussed in Chapter 5.[33] In this view of the common law, the rules are less characteristic of the process than are the "concrete instances from which they are drawn."[34] In contrasting the common law with the operation of law in continental legal systems, Pitkin relies on Edward Levi's conception of "reasoning by example" for her description of the common law. According to Levi, rules are remade in each instance of their use. The theory suggested here, however, of how ordinary language operates shows the inappropriateness of this idea that "rules are remade." The view of interpretation derived from the use of language rather than from a theory of reasoning suggests that interpretation is "legal" not because of the position of the judges, but because the judicial decision is based on conventions which comprise a legal "form of life."

Thomas Kuhn has made a similar revision of what was commonly held to be "science" by seeing it as an activity.[35] Kuhn argues against the traditional view of science as a systematic body of knowledge, regarding the activity of the practicing scientist, rather than the body of scientific knowledge, as characteristic of science. In a similar way, the linguistic model frees the conception of law from a strict identification with a body of rules distinct from the activity in which they are used.

Learning "steering mechanisms" is essential to the use of legal language in judicial interpretation. An exploration of this kind of learning by Gilbert Ryle provides some insight into the psycholinguistic aspects of judicial interpretation.[36] Ryle considers it inappropriate to view the ability to apply rules in practice as a mere habit. He distinguishes the ability to give the answers to multiplication problems by rote from the ability to solve them by calculating: "It is the essence of merely habitual practices that one performance is a replica of its predecessors. It is of the essence of intelligent practices that one performance is modified by its predecessors. The agent is still learning."[37] Ryle concludes that habits are learned by drill, while intelligent capacities are built up by training.

What it means to be "trained" is clarified by a description of the dispositional qualities which result from training. To be disposed toward some activity is not, according to Ryle, necessarily to do it at any given time, but is rather "to be bound or liable to be in a particular state, or to undergo a particular change, when a particular condition is realized."[38] Ryle suggests that training in language enables us to handle new contexts. In similar fashion, as a trained professional, the judge may be said to have a disposition to be influenced in his view of the world by his training in the language of law. Although he may not always manifest the disposition, it is a consideration which is likely to arise whenever he is dealing in the context in which the practices he knows through legal language are being considered.

The prior dispositions traditionally identified as functioning in judicial interpretation have been personal. The role of law has been seen in ideal terms as submerging the personal in favor of the legal. Law, in this sense, is considered as a constraint on human dispositions. Recognition of the linguistic characteristics of legal training may lead to a reexamination of the principles governing legal interpretation. Delmar Karlen has suggested that the power of precedent lies in principles that are more than uniquely legal. For him, these principles are (a) that one person ought to be treated like another under similar circumstances and (b) that there is no sense in working out fresh solutions for the same problem each time it occurs.[39] The point is restated by Julius Stone: "With or without *stare decisis*, judges still by and large attend to the experience of their predecessors, using comparable prior cases as guides to relevant principles and policies, rather than mere pegs on which to hang decisions."[40] Communication in language is only possible because there is reliance on established procedures. Whether or not they are viewed as compulsive, prior decisions serve as guides. They are not all the Justices have, of course, but they are the key to legal questions, the basis for the initial interpretation. To paraphrase Stanley Cavell, the Justices learn constitutional language and the unique world it delineates together.[41]

THE LIMITS OF LOGIC

According to Edward Levi, rules change from case to case where judges are at work. He suggests that this manner of reasoning is used chiefly in those cases where justification is sought for the adoption of new normative positions.[42] Levi's position integrates the necessarily creative processes in appellate interpretation with a theory of reasoning by example. However, his view does not adequately explain the relation between creativity and consistency which is critical to eliminating the dichotomy between the study of law and the behavior of judges. The linguistic model of "going on," on the other hand, suggests a description of creativity which integrates these traditionally disparate elements.

A characteristic of rule-governed behavior revealed by the investigations of ordinary language philosophers lies in the limited utility of logic in explaining "going on" to a new situation. The final step in a decision, drawing an inference, is something that cannot itself be represented in logical form.[43] Winch proposes that "learning to infer is learning to do something"[44] rather than merely learning the proper procedures. Linguistic operations are thus tied to particular actions rather than to justifications that are brought forth in support of the actions taken.

Formulating a sentence that is appropriate in a novel situation is a case of engaging in a practice conditioned by prior examples.[45] It is not ultimately tied to reasons or rules, for as Wittgenstein states, "reasons will soon give out. And then I shall act without reasons."[46] When compulsion is strong enough, action follows. Such action is more important than the reasons. Wittgenstein sees reasons and justification for an activity as less significant than the action itself. The experience or training that enables a child to speak is one which "gets him to go on." This encouragement is described as a "gesture meaning to 'go on like this'" and pointing beyond the examples given.[47] In the appellate judicial process, the necessity of choice is an institutional requirement.

An emphasis on action as the outcome of a decision follows from the position that reason cannot ultimately explain why something is done. The issue was discussed by Wittgenstein in his *Blue and Brown Books*:

> If you ask "why," do you ask for the cause or for the reason? If you ask for the cause, it is easy enough to think up a physiological or psychological hypothesis which explains the choice under the given conditions. It is the task of the experimental sciences to test such hypotheses. If on the other hand you ask for a reason the answer is, "There need not have been a reason for the choice."[48]

Through scientific investigations, we might find further explanation for a particular choice. Science will not, however, be able to give the reasons why someone made a choice.

Reasons are of little help in explaining the judicial decision because ultimately they will fail us. What, for instance, would satisfy the question *why*? What would stand as the final link between judicial action and a particular decision on an issue of constitutional law? The opinion traditionally links the decision to accepted lines of reasoning, but we can never be sure of the connection because of the nature of human action.[49] Wittgenstein wants to eliminate the notion of mental processes at this crucial point and suggest rather something like an automatic response. In his view, "the image which is brought up by the word is not arrived at by a rational process."[50] Such a claim would only push the description of the decision back further. What constitutes the calling up of conceptual possibilities and the assessment of their relevance, if not the experience that certain kinds of events fit into certain categories?

We are generally not content with such a limited explanation, and in explaining, we often seek to justify. Although such justifications do not really tell us "why" an action was taken, they may serve another function by revealing the relevant forms which an action may take. When a Justice writes an opinion, this explanation of the decision may be seen as a justification for the position taken rather than an elaboration of the basis upon which the decision was reached. Those who have applied some related facets of communication theory to judicial interpretation suggest that opinions are justifications for the decision in an effort to gain support.[51] The distinction between justifications and causes of actions in the philosophy of language allows the full potential of such theories to be appreciated.

While conventions, based in a social context, are the referents which must in principle be related to the use of language, there is no way to compel that linguistic guidelines be satisfied. In most cases experience will be followed as a matter of course. In difficult cases in language, as in law, the decision to go on is an action which cannot be bound to its justification.[52] Although reasons are significant considerations, they are necessarily of limited explanatory power.[53] The interpretation process is not governed by its justification. At the appellate level, the nature of the decision is not contained in the reasons but in the action.

Much work on the explanation of the nature of actions in the context of decision-making has been done with reference to law. The important contributions of John Wisdom, which have been influential, derive from the insights he gives into the function of context proposed by ordinary language philosophy. In regard to the degree to which belief is more like an action than a logical operation, Wisdom describes the use of argument as being characterized not by a "chain of demonstrative reasoning. . . . It is a presenting and representing of those features of the case which severally cooperate in favor of the conclusion. . . . The reasons are like the legs of a chair, not the links of a chain."[54] Other recent developments in this area have also relied on the discussion of rhetorical as opposed to logical argumentation and decision-making.[55]

Perelman's theories offer a similar position dealing with the nature and function of argument. His position supports developments in the philosophy of language. His work is also closely related to the arguments of Wisdom and Toulmin. H.L.A. Hart has noted the degree of affinity that Perelman's position has with the one developed thus far, proposing that what Perelman considers legal reasoning "makes an appeal less to universal logical principles than to certain basic assumptions peculiar to the lawyer." The assumptions are learned and operate through precedent and analogy. Hart views this kind of decision as "rational and yet not in the logical sense conclusive."[56] Perelman suggests that characterization of reasoning should be expanded in order to better reflect the influence of contextual considerations which often serve as the basis of proofs. The deductive proofs of formal logic are simply "foreign to the way in which . . . problems of social communication present themselves."[57] Rationality need not be confined to logic. What makes sense is often indicated by the grammar of our language, and these considerations operate as if prior to the rules of logic.

For Julius Stone, the "rhetorical" properties of legal argumentation are clearly as important as the logical. When judges defend legal "certainty" by claiming that it can be attained by simply sticking closely to the logical development of principles of law that already exist, they are basing their claim on a type of activity that has never existed. Instead, he proposes the following:

The working out of legal rules . . . is a creative adaption of law to changing social conditions. In this adaption, of course, deduction from existing principles of law plays some part, but deduction from non-legal premises found by judicial experience, and choice among competing legal principles and non-legal premises, or choices within a range of indeterminacy play a far more decisive one.[58]

This process of "arguing out" a problem rather than proceeding by means of deduction has been called dialectical reasoning. Its importance for the judicial decision has been emphasized by a number of scholars as being particularly appropriate to those cases where no clear legal precedent is available.[59]

Stone presents extensive documentation for the position that judicial interpretation is closer to contextual or rhetorical argument than to logical processes. ". . . in induction the accumulation of data usually allows fair prediction of 'what is to come,' but this may in juristic reasoning be open until the very moment of choice."[60] The reliance on induction is the key to this process of argumentation. The proposition that judicial decision-making can be explained partially in terms of linguistic capacities is similar to dialectical reasoning in that it emphasizes action on the basis of prior experience rather than rules. In my view, however, the contextual properties bearing on the decision are those of language rather than of argument. Nevertheless, there is a strong correlation between the two positions.

A related effort to clarify the way in which administrative discretion operates has been undertaken by Daniel J. Gifford. His approach begins with the contribution of ordinary language philosophy and has an immediate bearing on the operation of discretion in the judicial decision as discussed in this chapter.[61] Gifford finds that informal and largely internal constraints may be operable in decision-making. He refers to these constraints as "decisional referents."[62] In Gifford's study, language is used as a model for the reasoning process at work in administrative decision-making. The concern is with the validity of the appearance of discretion where rules do not determine the outcome of the case.[63] In examining this situation, Gifford draws support from Ronald Dworkin's assertion that an official who confronts rule ambiguity is most frequently obliged to resolve the ambiguity in accordance with "principles" or other guides furnished by the legal system.[64]

Gifford makes a distinction between "core" and "penumbral" areas of discretion,[65] a distinction which is drawn from investigation in ordinary language philosophy.[66] In the core areas, when the facts are clear and there is a governing rule, the content of the decision is said to be highly predictable. However, where the decision is ambiguous, falling in the penumbral area, the decision-maker may still not feel entirely free to decide in a purely personal way: "He may feel himself bound to decide in accordance with the principles, rules, goals, and so forth, which the system has supplied to him."[67] This notion of decisional referents remains rather abstract, but it emphasizes the significance for interpretive behavior of considerations in addition to rules. In administrative agencies, it is proposed that specialized bodies of knowledge form the background of the decisions handed down.[68] These bodies of knowledge may be as significant to the ultimate decision as the rules which are most clearly applicable.

This chapter has proposed that because judicial interpretation may be seen as behavior governed by principles of language use, the factors that influence interpretation in language bear on interpretation in law. Some mention of the differential impact at various levels of the legal system is warranted, although full consideration of the issues raised is beyond the scope of this work. It has been argued, for instance, that for the "great body of non-constitutional litigation there are standards which control judicial discretion."[69] Here, the variance among cases is less significant, and the guidance of prior practice can be taken to have a greater bearing on the outcome.[70] The process of "going on" at the trial level may not be essentially different from the appellate level, in that both involve interpretive judgment and action. The level of the legal structure merely alters the authoritative element in judicial interpretation. Thus, the bearing of the application in the lower courts on interpretation throughout the system is minimal. At the appellate level, it has been suggested that the decision does not involve an element of discretion which is unique to law. What is unique to the appellate level is the authoritative nature of high court choices, i.e., the significance in the Anglo-American system of a hierarchy of judicial authority. The result is that the opinions of the highest courts have a greater bearing on the grammar of the language of constitutional law than those of the lower courts.

Principles derived from the study of language are not new to the study of law. H.L.A. Hart, for example, is indebted to J. L. Austin for his discussion of the difference between convergent behavior and behavior according to rules. Austin's influence also appears in Hart's exploration of the varieties of imperatives in law.[71] John Rawls has also contributed to the study of law with a discussion based on Austinian principles.[72] The work of Austin and the Oxford school has been more compatible with traditional legal positivism than the work of Wittgenstein. This compatibility is based on a mutual emphasis on the rules governing speech activity and Austin's study of isolated "acts" in which words are used. I have chosen to elaborate the Wittgensteinian approach because I feel its utility in the study of law has yet to be recognized. I shall merely suggest the reasons for distinguishing what I take to be the contribution of Wittgenstein's formulation from the more established, but limited, applicability of Austin's.[73]

The contribution generally attributed to Austin is his distinction between "performative" and "constative" utterances. This distinction has been useful in elaborating the qualities of a particular "speech act." The notion of the "performative" suggests that to say something is in certain cases to do something, as when we say "I name this ship 'Liberte,'" or "I do" in a marriage ceremony. Hence, the performance of an action is completed in the utterance of a sentence, suggesting a relation between language and activity. The language of the law is full of performative concepts such as "offer and acceptance," "conveyance," or "deed."

Austin also teaches that too much is made of the supposed descriptive function of words. An example is the case where we believe that "knowing" describes a special state of mind. As Passmore explains, "To claim to know is not to describe my state but to make a plunge—to give others my word, my authority for saying that S is P."[74]

Interesting connections between Austin's view on words and the operations of the law have been and may still be made. But as Stone notes, it is excessive to claim that mere sharpened awareness of words can make "an essay on analytical jurisprudence simultaneously into one on descriptive sociology."[75] Austin's work is indeed more limited than Wittgenstein's in that it makes too much out of words and too little out of the structure of language. Walter Probert is critical of the aspects of legal positivism which reflect the Austinian view of language. He sees in legal positivism "an implicit faith in the way words serve as the medium for rules and laws, or in effect if not perception, how words do things to people. The implicit stress is on the inhibiting, conditioning side of words and language."[76] It is going on in new situations with constitutional language that characterizes judicial decisions where the precedent is not clear. Yet, these cases are not unlike ordinary cases in their reliance on prior experience; they are simply curious given the propensity to see the judicial decision as governed by precise formula.

NOTES

1. Walter Probert, *Law, Language and Communication*, p. 53.
2. Bernard Harrison, *Meaning and Structure*, p. 231.
3. Wittgenstein, *Philosophical Investigations*, par. 154.
4. *Roe v. Wade*, 410 U.S. 113 (1973).
5. Wittgenstein, *Philosophical Investigations*, par. 216.
6. Ibid., par 155; see also par. 151–153.
7. Ibid., par. 179.
8. Ibid., par. 198.
9. Ibid., par. 199.
10. Stephen Wasby, *Continuity and Change* (Pacific Palisades, Calif.: Goodyear Publishing Co., 1976), p. 111.
11. Barry Stroud, op. cit., p. 463.
12. Ibid.
13. J.F.M. Hunter, "Wittgenstein on Meaning and Use," in Klemke, op. cit., p. 391.
14. Wittgenstein, *Philosophical Investigations,* par. 199.
15. Ibid., see par. 208.
16. Pitkin, op. cit., p. 48.
17. Winch, op. cit., p. 45.
18. Ibid, p. 35.
19. Stanley Cavell, *Must We Mean What We Say?*, p. 52.
20. Anthony Lewis, *Gideon's Trumpet* (New York: Vintage Books, 1964), p. 34.
21. 372 U.S. 335
22. Julius Stone, *Legal System and Lawyer's Reasonings* (Stanford, Calif.: Stanford University Press, 1964), p. 23.
23. Probert, *Law, Language and Communication*, p. 37.
24. Ibid., p. 38.
25. Ibid., p. 47.
26. Stone, *Legal System,* p. 23.
27. Karl Renner, *The Institutions of Private Law and Their Social Function*, edited with an introduction and notes by O. Kahn-Freund (London: Routledge and Kegan Paul, 1949), p. 13.
28. Ibid.
29. Alf Ross, *On Law and Justice* (London: Stevens and Sons, Ltd., 1958), p. 327.
30. Probert, *Law, Language and Communication*, p. 15.
31. Edgar Bodenheimer, "A Neglected Theory of Legal Reasoning," *Journal of Legal Education* 21 (1969).

32. Wittgenstein, *Blue and Brown Books*, p. 81.

33. Pitkin, op. cit., p. 71.

34. Ibid., p. 55.

35. Thomas Kuhn, *The Structure of Scientific Revolutions* (Chicago: University of Chicago Press, 1962).

36. Gilbert Ryle, *The Concept of Mind* (New York: Barnes and Noble, 1949).

37. Ibid., p. 142.

38. Ibid., p. 43; see also Judith Shklar, *Legalism* (Cambridge, Mass.: Harvard University Press, 1964).

39. Delmar Karlen, *The Citizen in Court* (New York: Holt, Rinehart and Winston, 1964), p. 8.

40. Stone, *Legal System,* p. 333.

41. Cavell, *Must We Mean What We Say?*, p. 19.

42. Edward Levi, *An Introduction to Legal Reasoning* (Chicago: University of Chicago Press, 1958).

43. F. Waismann, "Verifiability," reprinted in *Logic and Language*, ed. Anthony Flew (New York: Doubleday and Co., 1965).

44. Winch, op. cit., p. 57.

45. Roger Brown, *Monographs of the Society for Research in Child Development*, Vol. 29, No. 1 (Chicago: University of Chicago Press, 1964).

46. Wittgenstein, *Philosophical Investigations,* par. 211.

47. Ibid., par. 208.

48. Wittgenstein, *Blue and Brown Books*, pp. 88, 110-111.

49. Ibid., p. 38.

50. Ibid., p. 89.

51. M. Shapiro, "Toward a Theory of Stare Decisis,"p. 125.

52. Winch, op. cit., p. 38.

53. Waismann, "Language Strata," reprinted in Flew, op. cit.

54. John Wisdom, *Philosophy and Psycho-analysis* (Berkeley: University of California Press, 1969), p. 157.

55. Chaim Perelman, op. cit.; Stephen Toulmin, *Uses of Argument;* Julius Stone, *Legal System*, p. 323ff.

56. H.L.A. Hart, "Introduction," in Perelman, op. cit., p. vii.

57. Perelman, op. cit., p. 152.

58. Stone, *Legal System*, p. 323.

59. Levi; Bodenheimer; and Jerome Hall, *Living Law of Democratic Society* (Indianapolis, Ind.: Bobbs-Merrill Co., 1949).

60. Stone, *Legal System*, p. 327.

61. Daniel J. Gifford, "Decisions, Decisional Referents and Admini-

strative Justice," *Law and Contemporary Problems* 37 (Winter 1972).

62. Ibid., p. 2.

63. Ibid., p. 5.

64. Ronald Dworkin, "The Model of Rules," pp. 36–46; "Social Rules and Legal Theory," *Yale Law Journal* 81 (1972): 855–879.

65. Gifford, op. cit., p. 6.

66. Waismann, "Verifiability," reprinted in Flew, op. cit.; see also Gifford, "Communication of Legal Standards," *Cornell Law Review* 56 (1971): 426–430.

67. Gifford, op. cit., p. 9.

68. Ibid., p. 17. See also Herbert Simon, *Administrative Behavior*, 2nd ed. (New York: Macmillan, 1957), pp. 169–170.

69. James L. Blawie and Marilyn J. Blawie, "The Judicial Decision: A Second Look at Certain Assumptions of Behavioral Research," *Western Political Quarterly* 18 (1965): 579–593.

70. Harold Spaeth, *An Introduction to Supreme Court Decision-Making*, revised ed. (San Francisco: Chandler, 1972), p. 56.

71. H.L.A. Hart, *The Concept of Law*, p. 9.

72. John Rawls, "Two Concepts of Rules," pp. 3–32.

73. J.L. Austin, op. cit., Lectures VIII-XII.

74. John Passmore, *A Hundred Years of Philosophy* (Baltimore: Penguin Books, 1957), p. 454.

75. Stone, *Legal System*, p. 10.

76. Probert, *Law, Language and Communication*, p. 7.

8 | Sense, Criteria, and Privacy

Most of those who have applied methods from the study of language to the law have hoped to improve the latter. Even those who have concentrated on logical analysis have suggested that it might raise the level of legal argument. One recent suggestion has held that the application of linguistic insights might improve the expressions of the Justices much as the study of grammar in the primary grades is meant to improve the writing ability of children.[1] Notwithstanding the fact that grammar generally has been employed to impose a particular form of speech and writing on those who in most cases could already communicate, in this investigation the goal is simply the description of judicial decision. The claim that there is a constitutional language and that it is different from ordinary language has political implications significant enough on their own without entering into a debate about the proper form of that constitutional language. The effort here is to show how tradition operates to structure decision. It is hoped that further research on this conceptual model will reveal the relation of legal language to ideology in general and thus better explain the way modes of thought benefit particular interests.

Yet, even at this point, we may explore the characteristics of interpretation based on the constitutional tradition. In this regard there are two relevant aspects of constitutional language, sense and criteria. In recent years, linguists have concentrated on precise description of language use. The result has been a method based on "what it makes sense to say" which explores the nature of well-formed statements by comparing them with ill-formed or nonsensical ones. The method is strangely alien to the other social sciences. Only where the researcher steps outside the struggles within his own culture has the attempt to understand a body of concepts been successful. This perspective has been distinctly lacking in political science due to its dependence on the investigation of processes that are dominated by highly charged issues. The first section of this chapter views sense in the constitutional tradition after a model of linguistic investigation.

Ordinary language philosophers have not been noted for the rigor of their analysis. Rather, they have labored in pursuit of insight into the nature of meaning. This lack of rigor has not been a major problem since the present study was not undertaken in order to provide an analysis of appropriate decisions based on the Constitution. Philosophers, however, have not entirely avoided the elements of rigorous description. In describing various states in language, grammar tells us how to proceed. But to understand the grammar of these states which our language enables us to describe, Wittgenstein proposes that we must ask "What counts as a criterion for any one's (or anything's) being in such a state?"[2] The discussion of the place of criteria in language use is as close as Wittgenstein comes to discussing the elements of particular linguistic acts. In ordinary language, "criteria" are the considerations which the user of a language relies on to determine what it does and does not make sense to say.

It is worthwhile to discuss both the nature of sense and criteria in language and to apply this discussion to a constitutional concept in order to indicate some of the things it reveals about judicial decision. The issue of when some event is a case of some constitutional concept is evident in the Justice's decision to decide, the discussion in oral argument, and the writing of an opinion. Sense, as revealed in ill-formed statements which show some of the formulations not possible, and criteria which bear on what stands as a case of something, are two facets of language that may be used to apply language analysis to the Constitution. This chapter views cases dealing with the concept of privacy and gives some attention to their dependence on sense and criteria.

CONSTITUTIONAL SENSE

As with ordinary language, the analysis of "ill-formed" or nonsensical statements serves to explicate the nature of constitutional intelligibility. The following observations are based on statements using concepts that have been dealt with in American courts in a constitutional setting. There are innumerable matters that do not make sense in constitutional law because they raise issues or rely on concepts that are not available in American constitutional language (e.g., mixed tribunals, divine right, alienation, or surplus value). Their use is a matter related to a larger issue of ideological constraints. However, at this point, in introducing the study of symbols in law, the traditional notion of sense arising from a linguistic context deserves limited treatment. The data to which these statements are subjected are therefore the decisions of the Supreme Court. In addition to showing some of the limits imposed by the constitutional tradition, the analysis shows how different classes of concepts function. Structure, as investigated here, involves abstract covering rights such as equal protection, explicit rights against the powers of government like the limits on search and seizure, the specific provisions of constitutional authority such as the power to regulate commerce, and satellite concepts like "illicit articles" emerging from the conflict over other provisions in the document. Their sense is derived from judicial interpretation. It goes beneath particular holdings, treating the opinions as revealing the structure in constitutional law. Following a convention in linguistics, statements that are ill-formed are marked with an asterisk (*).

The statement

*(1) Equal protection prohibits unreasonable searches

does not make constitutional sense. It is not the sort of claim that would be raised by an accomplished lawyer for consideration by the Supreme Court, although in *in forma pauperis* petitions the Court may be confronted with such claims. The tradition of constitutional interpretation compels the Justices to consider such claims nonsense. Sense in this context depends on an understanding of the Constitution, just as sense in ordinary language depends on the capacity to use language as a form of communication. The ordinary meaning of "equal protection" does not itself preclude (1). Indeed, if it were not for the structure of the Constitution and the existence of certain other rights, the statement might make some sense. (But that is like saying if it were not for the Constitution, the statement would make sense.) It is because other rights, those of search and seizure and due process, are traditionally the appropriate grounds for prohibiting unreasonable searches that the statement is ill-formed.

In another statement

(2) Unreasonable searches restrict the regulation of interstate commerce

the concepts are brought together in a way that makes sense. Their sense is not dependent here on the state of congressional regulation. Whether Congress has passed regulatory measures that involve the regulation of interstate commerce, or whether the Court has held the Constitution to apply to such statutes, does affect the truth of the claim. The sense of (2) is dependent on the constitutional tradition. Unlike (1), there is no more appropriate concept or structural element in the Constitution that would preclude such an application. The Fourth Amendment right, in its application to the federal government, may at some point cover an exercise of this power in the realm of commerce. There is no reason, in the tradition of use, why the Fourth Amendment might not be applied in this way. The openness of the categories to this connection depends on the fact that federal power is limited by fundamental constitutional rights.

One of the traditional limits on the use of equal protection is its application to state rather than private action. This is a unique aspect of constitutional language, as anyone who has tried to convey it to students of the Constitution is aware. As a result of this tradition, it would not make sense to claim that

*(3) My neighbor's refusal to invite me to his party on account of my sex violates my constitutional right to equal protection of the laws.

This is the sort of claim to a basic right that an ordinary citizen might well wish to make. Certainly similar, though less clearly ill-formed, statements like those that might surround instances of racial discrimination in rental housing intuitively suggest a constitutional ground. But an equal protection claim to the Constitution is appropriate only if the state is implicated. Although the reach of state implication has broadened considerably in the last two decades, it is not close to statement (3) —not if the party is an ordinary social gathering in a private home.

On the other hand, although it may be bewildering to those not

conversant with constitutional development, the following statement makes sense in constitutional terms:

> (4) The refusal of a private club, which holds a liquor license, to
> serve me on account of my sex violates my right to equal pro-
> tection.

The tradition of interpretation bearing on (4) indicates that it makes
sense, whether or not the particular holdings at any given time
make it an accurate description of the law. The creativity of the
Warren Court in this area, as in commerce and search and seizure,
widened the sphere of possible interpretation, but the underlying
logic predates and indeed supports this development. The Justices
performed their wizardry with the tools available and in light of the
constraints of the Constitution.

As has been shown in the case of privacy, claims that may once
have made no sense can become intelligible. Thus,

> (5) The right to privacy prohibits states from making all abor-
> tions illegal

would have made no sense in 1873, but 100 years later, it was
authoritatively announced from the high bench. The law moves in
this way when an activity not normally covered can be conceived to
be within the bounds of intelligibility with regard to a claim.

This move is evident in the claim made by Clarence Earl Gideon
(as discussed in Chapter 6),

> (6) The Supreme Court guarantees me a right to counsel.

It was not only a sensible claim, but it came to be true following
the success of Gideon's appeal. The preceding discussion proposes
that before it was true, it was reasonable to extrapolate to the
claim from established understanding of the concepts. Unlike (1),
which is unintelligible, (6) would have been wrong prior to 1963,
but it was intelligible and hence the basis of a petition accepted by
the Court. An unintelligible claim in this area of law might involve
a request from a state to have the Supreme Court appoint counsel
for its response to a criminal appeal such as that filed by Gideon.
An even more interesting prospect, however, is the range of intelligibility evident in the right to counsel cases. *Betts v. Brady*[3]
had established that the right to counsel existed where special circumstances warranted it. *Gideon v. Wainwright*[4] expanded the
law to include all felony prosecutions. *Argersinger v. Hamlin*[5]
developed the right still further to include all prosecutions where

there was a threat of imprisonment. The underlying logic is, of course, that ordinary citizens would not be able to successfully handle the legal technicalities of a trial. The system requires that a defendant have trained counsel available to guide him through the legal maze. Not only does the very logic of these cases support the notion that there is a distinct legal sphere that even a wise man cannot penetrate without proper training, but also the evolution of these holdings suggests the nature of the evolution of intelligibility in the law. It is doubtful that the sensibilities evident in 1972 in *Argersinger* would have had grounds for expression in 1942 when *Betts* was decided. It may be further suggested that the notion of fairness and equal protection that underlie the evolution from *Betts* to *Argersinger* would still not be able to support a claim that one has a right to the best lawyer that money can buy—although the provisions of such necessities as expenses for attorney's fees or funds to pay for the subsistence of witnesses are not beyond the vision of the Justices. Here it is perhaps not the structure of the Constitution that stands as a limitation but the underlying ideological limitation of a market economy that still tolerates vast inequities in wealth. The limitations on constitutional sense are not only in the Constitution, but the description of constitutional limitations of this sort is a step toward demonstrating the ideological ones, as was indicated in the introduction to this chapter.

While the preceding examples rely on the words of the document, the investigation may be expanded by looking at concepts developed in working with the basic provisions and rights. A class of concepts bearing on constitutional adjudication has been referred to as "satellite concepts."[6] These concepts represent interpretations of the written Constitution in light of the conflicts that have arisen over it. Although the underlying structural relations bear on the development of these concepts, the contribution of this notion in the present context is the identification of a class of concepts which develop out of constitutional conflict. "Moral pestilence" delineates a concept that has evolved as covered by the congressional right to regulate commerce. "Moral pestilence" as a concept facilitated the constitutional justification of the Mann Act.

The satellite categories are interpretive tools which also depend on relations with other concepts for their meaning. Hence, the statement

(7) Congress may not regulate illicit articles unless they are part of interstate commerce

makes sense given the understanding that such articles are within the scope of the commerce power. On the other hand, the statement

*(8) Congress may regulate illicit articles unless they are part of interstate commerce

does not make sense. Since the concept expresses a limited dimension of a power granted to Congress, it has no meaning except in the exercise of that power. In this case, interstate commerce is a realm into which Congress can enter with qualifications, and illicit articles are some of the things that allow such entry. It is not simply false to suggest that illicit articles cannot be regulated when they are part of interstate commerce. Rather, since the concept was introduced as a factor in that sphere, such a statement makes no sense. Similarly, the following statement

*(9) The extent of congressional involvement with state problems is dependent on its regulation of illicit articles

is ill-formed because it misstates the function of the satellite category which articulates a congressional power in a restricted sphere. Its dependence on interstate commerce is missing here in a more expansive claim than the sense of the Constitution can carry.

Particular concepts can thus be said to have a meaning acquired through use and to depend on the tradition of constitutional interpretation for appropriate application. In examining this tradition, it has been helpful to indicate different ways that concepts relate to a conceptual structure. Whether these ways are the most significant is a matter for further study. They are mentioned here as an outgrowth of the effort to show the existence of structures governing intelligible constitutional discourse.

CONCEPTUAL CRITERIA

In ordinary discourse, we are likely to be confident in a judgment that the familiar house pet that meows and chases birds deserves to be called a "cat." We would expect nothing else to be the case. But if this animal began to talk, or even bark, doubt would certainly arise as to the proper terminology to apply to it. As in the discussion of linguistic interpretation, linguistic capacities must be clear enough to reveal normal patterns, yet flexible enough to allow new considerations to be handled. Similar situations arise in constitutional law. For instance, the employment of thumbscrews or the rack to obtain a confession would not fall within the conventional requirement that a confession be "voluntary." Other methods, such as "custodial interrogration," present more difficult problems for interpretation of the Constitution.[7] The first example suggests the extent to which constitutional language is socially based. It is cases like those involving "custodial interrogation" that make their way to the Court and have a chance of being reviewed. The sense of the constitutional protections includes the idea that confessions be voluntary. We understand this when the elements of constitutional concepts have been acquired. Wittgenstein proposes that we call these elements "criteria."

Wittgenstein never fully developed the notion of criteria, but there is some indication of what he had in mind and considerable philosophical controversy over the issue. The concern with criteria focuses on how we know that something which we encounter is a case of something which we know. Wittgenstein suggested that we sometimes make such judgments in terms of "criteria" and sometimes in terms of what he called "symptoms."

Wittgenstein explained what he meant by "criteria" by means of an example from medicine:

If medical science calls angina an inflammation caused by a particular bacillus, and we ask in a particular case "why do you say this man has got angina?" then the answer "I have found the bacillus so-and-so in his blood" gives us the criterion, or what we call the defining criterion of angina.[8]

He further explains that to say "A man has angina if this bacillus is found in him" is a tautological proposition as well as a loose way of stating the definition of angina. Criteria are the considerations in terms of which a definition is given. For confessions, the interrogation must not be of a form that would lead to involuntary self-incrimination. The logic and structure of the law require that any confession to a crime be of the defendant's own accord. The Court's holdings are explained in the language of the tautological proposition. A confession is unconstitutional if it is involuntary.

According to Wittgenstein, a "symptom" of something, on the other hand, is "a phenomenon of which experience has taught us that it coincided, in some way or other, with the phenomenon which is our defining criterion."[9] The relation of a "symptom" to something is hypothetical. That is, to say "A man has angina whenever he has an inflamed throat" is to make a hypothesis.[10] Symptoms are the clues on the basis of which we might hypothesize that such and such is the case. In the case of interrogations, since 1897[11] the Court has held that physical or mental coercion is an unconstitutional means for securing confessions. Such aspects of the interrogation as "continuous questioning," "incommunicado confinement," and "unnecessary delay" have been viewed as the symptoms by which the Court has in recent years recognized unconstitutional methods of obtaining confessions.[12] Thus, to say that a confession is involuntary when there is incommunicado confinement is to make a hypothesis, as the Court does when it assumes that some intervening evidence that the testimony is reliable would allow a confession to stand.[13]

I am concerned with "criteria" in this investigation since they are the key to the meaning of language. An understanding of their qualities and their relation to meaning indicates the nature of the grammatical relations in language. The criteria are elements of any concept that characterize its place in the scheme of practices. Since they are embedded in the system of use, the evolution of the criteria for concepts is quite deliberate. "Symptoms," on the other hand, do not reveal linguistic properties so much as our insight into different states of affairs. It is such dimensions of concepts that are in a more constant state of flux in constitutional interpretation.

Following Wittgenstein's example of a toothache, criteria become part of the "use" or "grammar" of the word "toothache": "One behaving in such a way decides the question whether he has a toothache or not . . . this behavior . . . is a matter of 'definition' a convention.''[14] Commentary on this position has suggested that "the criterion for a thing being so" is the "primary phenomenon by which one may judge that it is so.''[15] Criteria are noninductive pieces of evidence for thinking that something is so. The close relationship between the criteria and the thing defined characterizes criteria as *a priori* reasons for believing something to be so. In the case of the word "pain," for example, the criteria are what we learn as we learn the word "pain," i.e., the pain behavior.

A strong relation has been proposed between meaning and criteria, while philsophers have stipulated that the existence of criteria is not a necessary condition for the existence of the thing to which the criteria refer.[16] These interpretations consider the example in which a certain bacillus in the blood is a defining criterion of angina. According to John Canfield, they suggest the following view of criteria: " 'X is the criterion of Y' means that it is true in virtue of a definition, convention, or rule of language that if X then Y.''[17] Criteria are evident in definitions, conventions, or rules of language. In the example which Canfield explores, the criterion for calling a square of a certain color "R" is that the color of the square matches the color on a chart which is used for making such ascriptions. In this example, the chart, when used to ascribe the symbol "R" to color, is employed much as rules of language are employed. Rules of language can be explicit or implicit. Following the example of the color chart, it may be that the chart is used at first to learn the language and is then discarded, or it may be that activities when observed, though following no such chart, can be described with reference to such a chart.

In this reading of Wittgenstein, the presence of criteria is a sufficient condition for what they stand as criteria of but not a necessary condition. Whenever the criteria are present, the concept which they define may be said to be present. But it would not be contradictory to assert, in a particular case, that although the criteria are present, the thing or concept for which they stand as criteria is not present. This is because the meaning relation between the criteria and the concept could not insure that a particular case is one where a person applying the concept is not being deceived.[18] Or, if not a case of deception, it may be a case in which other considerations arise which had not previously been recognized or considered. In law, this characteristic of criteria is particularly informative. As is developed in the subsequent discussion of privacy, the dissent from the application of a sensible concept depends on distinguishing the criteria of the concept from the circumstances in the particular case. The distinction can either be on the basis of the absence of the criteria or by indication that some other factor makes its application inappropriate in the case.

The concept "searches and seizures" derives its meaning from the experience of constitutional interpretation. It had traditionally been associated with "trespass" and "physical object" (see Chapter 6).[19] A theory incorporating technological developments evolved reflecting the limits of the traditional reliance on penetration. It required the support of a related concept. In order to say that a wiretap constitutes a "search and seizure," the Supreme Court, in *Katz v. U.S.*,[20] introduced the protection against self-incrimination. *Katz* exemplifies the process of conceptual development derived from experience, and it is evidence of constitutional flexibility. The room to maneuver is still constrained by the conceptual possibilities surrounding it. Given the development of a provision like "search and seizure" and the availability of a related concept like "self-incrimination," it made sense to claim that a wiretap was subject to constitutional protection, even though no such authoritative determination had been made prior to *Katz*. On the other hand, the sense of the concept as evident in the reliance on intrusion militates against its being used as a protection against something like the report of a public speech. There are limits on conceptual application that govern constitutional interpretation.

"Unreasonable searches and seizures" constitutes a practice in the activity of constitutional interpretation, i.e., in the use of constitutional language. The criteria for this practice can be seen in terms of the traditional trespass and physical object requirements. These criteria may change, but the changes cannot transcend the nature of the practices if they are to be intelligible. To say that a wiretap constitutes a search and seizure was a significant enough break from established practice that in *Katz* the Court found it appropriate to rely on the grammar of another concept, that of self-incrimination. An unwarranted physical intrusion into a home was for a long time sufficient for such an intrusion to constitute a constitutionally unreasonable search. The physical intrusion might in this case be considered a criterion for what is to constitute a search. The application of constitutional guarantees against unreasonable searches and seizures to a wiretap, however, expanded the conventional understanding of intrusion. Intrusion in the traditional sense of a physical penetration was no longer necessary, although the existence of such penetration remained sufficient. Wiretaps without authorization thus became symptoms of unwarranted searches and seizures as a result of the fact that physical penetration was no longer a criterion of the concept.

In elaborating the thesis that criteria are sufficient but not necessary conditions for something being the case, philosophers have resisted the position that there is an entailment between a statement that a criterion is present and that the corresponding thing necessarily exists.[21] The realm of Wittgensteinian grammar is an invitation to look at the use of words and not manufacture *a priori* theses about them.[22] Criteria are aids in this effort. To suggest that the existence of the criteria entailed the existence of the concept would be to manufacture such *a prioria*. According to Oldenquist, "explaining the grammar of a word is, roughly, explaining how it works. And given that he (Wittgenstein) is talking about grammar, there is no basis for grinding entailments or analytical truths out of this conceptual relationship."[23] Such rigidity of formulation is not characteristic of Wittgenstein's method. He does not provide arguments and proofs but rather, through metaphors, similes, and analogies, we are given to understand the characteristics of language use. Criteria, in this tradition, must be seen as tools for determining the conventions that constitute the "grammar" of language.

The grammar of linguistic concepts is derived from a background of circumstances.[24] The importance of this background is not something that is taught to the learners of a language, but rather something that obtains in teaching against the background of language. Background circumstances are the intervening factors between the criteria and the thing or concept for which something is a criterion. It is thus not necessary that if criterion "X" is present then "Y" follows, but rather, that if "X" is present and the background circumstances remain the same, then "Y." Given the nature of language, this role of criteria in the context of the governing principles of grammar is the key to the possibility of communication. It is not a rigid calculus, but a sort of operational tradition that represents how we go on with a language. When we learn to use linguistic concepts, the background does not tell all the circumstances that may arise. When new circumstances arise, it is essential that they are capable of being incorporated into the use of already existing concepts.

The view that criteria reveal concepts is thus compatible with the position that concepts are not tied to particular criteria. Criteria represent the definitions, conventions, and rules of the ordinary use of language. Yet, some additional characterisitc may appear, as is often the case in law, which had not been considered in the original conception. We can say much about concepts in ordinary language, as in law, without explicating the entire grammar of what is appropriate. This openness is a reason for employing modern linguistic theory to describe legal interpretation. "Criteria" is a useful tool in mapping the linguistic function. Philosophers have observed that it can be employed "to determine that something is the case," "to identify something," as well as "in the making of judgments," or "to justify a judgment."[25] All of these activities, which ultimately are governed by the grammar or sense of the legal tradition, can be observed in the operation of those who work with the law. In law, as in language, the criterion of something is the key to how we learn and continue to understand what it is. The relation of the criteria to the concept amplifies a crucial aspect of the interpretive process. It is this process which forms the basis of judicial decision, since the decision must ultimately be made up of the activities of determining, identifying, making, and justifying judgments.

CONSTITUTIONAL PRIVACY: THE USE OF A CONCEPT

Once established in the constitutional sphere, the use of a concept depends on sense and criteria. Whether the concept has emerged from specific provisions as with search and seizure or whether it is the product of a more creative introduction into constitutional adjudication, as with privacy, the use of the concept may be examined with reference to discussion of criteria. The following survey of recent privacy cases examines the criteria that have been evident. It further suggests that, while the judicial decision depends on the existence of a concept, it is not sufficient to guarantee a holding even where the criteria exist. In this sense, the decision to apply a concept differs fundamentally from the decision not to apply it.

In the decade following the *Griswold* decision, although privacy was appealed to as an independent constitutional right,[26] it was successful only where it was applied to the search and seizure context;[27] the privacy of the home;[28] or the realm of sexual or marital privacy.[29] These are the kinds of criteria that the concept may be said to have.

In *Eisenstadt,* the contraceptive situation was the basis for an extension that goes beyond the marital relationship. The opinion by Justice Brennan stated: "If the right of privacy means anything, it is the right of the individual, married or single, to be free from unwarranted governmental intrusion into matters so fundamentally affecting a person as the decision whether to bear or beget a child."[30] It is the fact that distribution is not banned to married persons that makes its denial to unmarried persons a violation of equal protection in the domain of privacy. Where the concept in *Griswold* elevated the "right to be let alone" to constitutional stature in the marital relationship, *Eisenstadt* provided the connection with the first abortion decision,[31] which raised the standard to one of "personal autonomy,"[32] albeit in a sphere closely related to previous holdings.

Of the subsequent holdings to deal with constitutional privacy, none more firmly demonstrated the new status of privacy than the 1973 abortion ruling, *Roe v. Wade.* In *Roe,* privacy not only received its fullest expression, but it was also referred to in a way that indicates the degree to which it had become a part of the Justices' tool box. Justice Blackmun seemed less concerned about the source of the right in his abortion opinion than about the fact that it was a recognized claim.

This right of privacy, whether it be founded in the Fourteenth Amendment's concept of personal liberty and restriction upon state action, as we feel it is, or, as the District Court determined, in the Ninth Amendment's reservation of rights to the people, is broad enough to encompass a woman's decision whether or not to terminate her pregnancy.[33]

It has been noted that the opinion treats the case as "just one of the many cases that recognized the right of privacy."[34]

Once a concept has emerged sufficiently to be an acknowledged part of the constitutional setting, the criteria upon which a particular application may be made can be examined. There is evidence of a shared experience and an intelligibility to the claim derived not from particular decisions but from groups of cases and the related reasoning. Justice Rehnquist held in dissent: "I have difficulty in concluding, as the Court does, that the right of 'privacy' is involved in this case. . . . Nor is the 'privacy' which the Court finds here even a distant relative of the freedom from searches and seizures."[35] Still later, a criterion previously established was offered by the majority as a limitation on exercise of the right. " . . . the Court has recognized that 'zones of privacy' may be created by more specific guarantees and thereby impose limits upon government power . . . . Respondent's case, however, comes within none of these areas."[36] Both cases could have been intelligibly related to the concept of privacy. Indeed, it is implicit in much that has been said up to this point that unintelligible claims are not very likely to be granted a full hearing by the Supreme Court. But the idea of criteria is relevant here, for it focuses attention on the subject of adjudication. In the process of avoiding the push of precedent, which is part of the constitutional tradition, the Justices may choose to distinguish a case before them from situations bearing on the use of the concept. In this activity, the elements of criteria are the subjects of argument and justification.

The structure to privacy, which is suggested by the stages of development and process of expansion, has a bearing on interpretative use of the concept. The long struggle for the establishment of a legal right reveals a fundamentally different kind of activity from that where a right might cease being actively used. Judicial interpretation is the process from which the objects of conflict emerge as well as the process in which the conflicts are resolved. The opinions of the Court reveal consciousness of these objects of conflict. Only objects so constituted as to be able to be presented as intelligible claims will arise. Opinions present clues to future objects (or concepts) in the same process through which they are resolved. The anticipation or expectation which is the response to opinions is directed toward the interpretive possibilities as well as the possibilities of a successful outcome.

Treatment of the constitutional right of privacy in judicial interpretation raises very difficult problems as to the nature of that process. Most legal scholars, although reflecting on developments in the law, pay scant attention to the impact of that developmental process, reserving their creative effort for prediction and advocacy. In addition, much of the literature on interpretation which is consistent with this treatment of legal concepts[37] is more attentive to the process of creation than to the limits on creativity. However, privacy, as interpreted in the previous cases, does impose limits. The limits are imposed by the meaning of the concept and the expectations it generates.

One of the first major refusals to expand the concept of privacy following *Roe v. Wade* came in 1974 on the issue of a zoning ordinance directed at unrelated persons living together.[38] The ordinance presented a case slightly outside of the dominant context of home, family, and sexual relations; it was brought on the expectation that a constitutional right had been violated, a result of past developments in the interpretation of privacy. That the Court chose to hear the case indicates that a number of Justices were interested in considering such an expansion. The claim was unsuccessful, but it reached the Court as a reasonable application of the concept of privacy. The traditional criteria seemed to be present, although the absence of a family relation may have been the significant factor in the decision.

Although the attention to privacy in the common law has been a key to constitutional development, common law applications have also been limited by constitutional protections. The clearest evidence of this sort of limitation is in reference to the First Amendment. While the First Amendment was relied on to establish the right of privacy in the Constitution, the common law right has always been at odds with the First Amendment. The appellants in *Cox Broadcasting Corporation v. Cohn* (1975)[39] and *Time, Inc. v. Firestone* (1970)[40] brought actions against the press for publication of information which they believed to violate rights traceable to the early protections of privacy. The Supreme Court held that the protections of the First and Fourteenth Amendments limited this privacy right. It is not insignificant in these cases that the Court went to considerable lengths to give credence to the importance of the right to privacy, while at the same time indicating that the common law right, when introduced into the constitutional setting, was limited by established guarantees in the Bill of Rights. The cases show an important structural element in the Constitution which never imposed the same limits in the common law development of privacy, the associational right of privacy or privacy of belief. It was in part these elements which gave the privacy in the Constitution greater breadth than in the common law. These attributes of the First Amendment were recently given extensive discussion in *Buckley v. Valeo* (1976).[41] Reliance was placed directly on the fundamental First Amendment relations and the "privacy of belief" in an important section of the opinion. Joined to the attributes found in the Fourth and Fifth Amendments, this aspect of privacy seems to have fostered a concept broader than the specific protections of the Bill of Rights.

Recent examples of the continuing authority of the right of privacy, the 1976 abortion cases,[42] simply maintained established dimensions of the concept. Justice Blackmun again treated privacy in the indicative mode; indeed, in these cases, even the right to have an abortion was dealt with in that mode. That right was accepted as the basis from which related matters such as the consent of the father, or the parents, was considered. Little was offered with regard to new expectations for the right. That the Court is still predisposed to consider past interpretations as worthy of support is important, but authoritative holdings constitute only part of constitutional discourse, and these cases seldom reveal anything new about the meaning of constitutional privacy.

At least for a time, the development of the right of privacy in the Constitution seems to have reached a peak. Instances of holding the line to the past rulings, refusing appeals, and articulating new limitations are already evident. But there is a fundamental difference between incorporation and erosion of the right. When introduced into a new place, it must somehow fit in that place. Not using a concept, however, does not present the same problems. Certain situations may create expectations out of a tradition of use, but an unfulfilled expectation is conceptually less abrasive (and more likely) than a nonsensical claim. This way of limiting the right to be let alone has involved relying on the liberty concept in the Fourteenth Amendment and interpreting it to include only those specific areas already protected by the right of privacy. Paradoxically, by moving to greater abstraction, the Court has been able to accept prior decisions while minimizing the broader implications arising from their incorporation in the privacy concept. It is one way of circumventing the concept. In *Kelley v. Johnson*, decided on April 5, 1976, Justice Rehnquist referred to claims against infringement on the "individual's freedom of choice with respect to certain basic matters of procreation, marriage, and family life" as having been given constitutional protection. He ignored any possibly greater scope, however: " . . . whether the citizenry at large has some sort of 'liberty' interest within the Fourteenth Amendment in matters of personal appearance is a question on which this Court's cases offer little, if any, guidance."[43] The matter at issue was the right of a police officer to determine the length of his hair. That privacy was involved in the case, though skirted in the majority opinion, is evident both in the references to the same cases that established that right and in the dissent by Justice Marshall which tied personal appearance to "the right to be let alone."[44] While the weight of the opinion rested on the special circumstances of the case, the effort by Justice Rehnquist to avoid the privacy issue was also evident. This is a different sort of activity from the process of conceptual growth. By substitution and exclusion, the meaning of a concept and its structure need not be confronted. But a concept may begin to sound strange, and expectations lapse as a result of disuse.

An instance of the Supreme Court's refusal to even hear a claim to a more expansive holding in the area of privacy occurred in 1976 in the case of *Doe v. Commonwealth's Attorney for the City of Richmond.*[45] In this case, a Federal District Court had upheld Virginia's law prohibiting private homosexual acts. By not hearing the appeal from the lower court, the Supreme Court affirmed the decision. The action produced considerable debate and revealed the force of public expectation generated by the right of privacy.[46] Three judges wished to hear the appeal, suggesting the possibility that they found it within the tradition of constitutional discourse. The boundaries of conceptual development on constitutional matters might be further refined by examining petitions for review by the Supreme Court which two or three Justices wish to hear.

In *Paul v. Davis,* decided on March 23, 1976, the Supreme Court considered a case in which a person who had been arrested for shoplifting and had the charges filed away found his name and picture on an "Active Shoplifters" flyer distributed throughout the community. Justice Rehnquist wrote in the opinion of the Court: "The Court has recognized that 'zones of privacy' may be created by more specific constitutional guarantees and thereby impose limits on government power. Respondent's case, however, comes within none of these areas."[47] He then went on to describe the "fundamental rights" protected by privacy and "declined to enlarge them" in the manner suggested by the case. In dissent, however, Justice Brennan asserted: " . . . privacy notions appear to be inextricably interwoven with the considerations which require that a state not single an individual out for punishment outside the judicial process."[48] In both the majority and the dissent, the concept of privacy was the object of interpretation. The concept was the link between the opinions, and it was shared, although its application was very much at issue. While the dissent was more in keeping with the evolution of the right, with its roots in the common law protection against disclosure, the majority was inclined to distinguish the application from that body of the interpretive tradition.

One of the most recent privacy cases in the Supreme Court, *Whalen v. Roe,*[49] reveals the way constitutional structure is available to the Justices to engage in a kind of reasoning that is deeper than that suggested by criteria. Here, the structural dimension is that evident in the other general liberties in the Bill of Rights. As Judge Knapp said in using this case, "the paramount issue . . . is not whether a right of privacy exists [in this case], but rather whether the record indicates that such a right will be abridged."[50] In *Whalen*, the Supreme Court had been asked to decide whether a New York statute requiring the names and addresses of persons who received certain prescribed drugs to be reported to the state was an intrusion on the right of privacy. Whatever the right of privacy meant, it was not that whenever it was found to apply to a case that case would involve a constitutional violation. Justice Stevens found invasions of privacy to be part of health care: "Requiring such disclosure to representatives of the state having responsibility for the health of the community, does not automatically amount to an impermissible invasion of privacy."[51] Stevens concluded that the threat was not sufficient to establish a constitutional violation. The structure of the constitutional tradition includes the idea that the police power is a basis for evaluating the constitutionality of state action, even when a constitutional right is involved. The police power is in the tradition of constitutional adjudication and thus serves as a justification for action. Suffice it to say that what makes sense here as part of the Constitution does not make sense to all concerned with the issues, particularly those for whom privacy is an absolute.

The decisions made in the Supreme Court are actions on a world at least partially constituted in the Justices' minds. In matters of intelligibility, it is easier to explore and explicate the structure that governs in situations where the concepts are used rather than when they are evaded. It is in use that the constraints are most evident and the expectations created. When concepts are not applied, they seem to be beyond the reach of the constraints, but the sense of an application in a particular area may still be compelling and expectations from past use provide a guide to possible alternatives. The value of examining the use of a concept such as "privacy" is in the demonstration of structural limits on use. From the recognition of the right at the constitutional level, and of its recent eclipse, certain traditions inform and legitimize the process at a level beneath the ebb and flow that dictates who wins and who loses. It is clearer here than in other arenas that the body of relevant conceptions is a key to substantive possibilities and particular outcomes because these concepts are what the struggles are over.

NOTES

1. Layman E. Allen, et al., *Communication Sciences and the Law* (Indianapolis, Ind.: Bobbs-Merrill Co., 1965).
2. Wittgenstein, *Philosophical Investigations*, par. 572. See also Pitkin, op. cit., p. 126.
3. 316 U.S. 455 (1942).
4. Op. cit.
5. 407 U.S. 25 (1972).
6. Levi, op. cit., pp. 60–70.
7. *Miranda v. Arizona*, 384 U.S. 436 (1966).
8. Wittgenstein, *Blue and Brown Books*, pp. 24–25.
9. Ibid.
10. Ibid.
11. *Bram v. U.S.*, 168 U.S. 532.
12. Pritchett, *The American Constitution*, pp. 448–450.
13. *Stein v. New York*, 346 U.S. 156 (1953).
14. Rogers Albritton, "On Wittgenstein's Use of the Term 'Criterion,'" in *Wittgenstein, The Philosophical Investigations,* ed. George Pitcher (New York: Anchor Books, 1966), p. 249.
15. Ibid., p. 237.
16. John V. Canfield, "Criteria and Rules of Language," *Philosophical Review* 1 (1974): 70–87.
17. Ibid., p. 71.
18. Andrew Oldenquist, "Wittgenstein on Phenomenalism, Skepticism, and Criteria," in Klemke, op. cit., p. 420.
19. *Silverman v. U.S.*, 365 U.S. 505 (1961).
20. 389 U.S. 347 (1967).
21. Canfield, op. cit., p. 73.
22. N. Malcolm, "Anselm's Ontological Argument," *Philosophical Review* 69 (1960): 389–394.
23. Oldenquist, op. cit., p. 422.
24. Canfield, op. cit., p. 78.
25. Ibid., p. 74.
26. *Paris Adult Theatre I v. Slaton*, 413 U.S. 49 (1973).
27. *Katz*, op. cit.

28. *Stanley v. Georgia*, 394 U.S. 557 (1969); *United States v. Reidel*, 402 U.S. 351 (1971).

29. *Eisenstadt v. Baird*, 405 U.S. 438 (1972).

30. Ibid., 453.

31. *Roe v. Wade*, 410 U.S. 113 (1973).

32. Gerald Gunther, *Cases on Constitutional Law* (Mineola, N.Y.: Foundation Press, 1976), p. 650.

33. *Roe*, op. cit., p. 153.

34. Richard A. Epstein, "Substantive Due Process by Any Other Name: The Abortion Cases," *Supreme Court Review* (Chicago: University of Chicago Press, 1973).

35. *Roe*, op. cit.

36. *Paul v. Davis*, 96 S. Ct. 1155 (1976).

37. Dworkin, *Taking Rights Seriously*; Stone, *Legal System and Lawyer's Reasonings;* Levi, op. cit.

38. *Village of Belle Terre v. Boraos,* 416 U.S. 1 (1974).

39. 420 U.S. 469 (1975).

40. 96 S. Ct. 958 (1970).

41. 96 S. Ct. 612 (1976).

42. *Planned Parenthood v. Danforth*, 96 S. Ct. 2831 (1976).

43. *Kelley v. Johnson*, 96 S. Ct. 1440 (1976), p. 1444.

44. Ibid., p. 1448.

45. 96 S. Ct. 1489 (1976).

46. Editorial, *New York Times*, March 31, 1976.

47. *Paul*, op. cit., p. 1166.

48. Ibid., p. 1177.

49. 429 U.S. 589 (1977).

50. *DuPont v. John F. Finklea*, U.S. Dist. Ct. for Southern District of West Virginia, December 20, 1977, p. 6.

51. Whalen, op. cit., p. 602.

9 | Conclusion: Symbols, Authority, and Legitimacy

A model of the judicial decision based on language rather than on rules or attitudes best portrays how students of politics may characterize the place of law in this situation. Rather than as rules, which are most significant for the ordinary citizen or the lower courts, conceptual structures constitute the greatest limitation on judicial action and thus distinguish the legal from the political sphere. Rather than as attitudes, which delineate the political inclinations that constitute choice among possible forms of action, conceptual structures operate as characteristics of the symbolic activity that we know as law.

This view is responsive to concerns expressed by critics of contemporary social science.[1] It is the meaning and structure of language that sets "the frame within which political thought and action proceed."[2] Attention to the decision, as bounded by language, focuses on the "intersubjective meanings" that Taylor[3] has seen as characteristic of social life. The phenomenological perspective is evident in Alfred Schutz's view that sensible claims in society are responsive to the "already constituted meanings of active participants in the social world."[4] The tradition of constitutional interpretation contains those meanings upon which the action that constitutes judicial decision is based.

The way these meanings have operated in the legal sphere has not gone unacknowledged by students of the judiciary. Indeed, ten years ago two prominent figures suggested the need for renewed attention to the meanings shared by the judges. The suggestions were offered as a counter to the emphasis on political factors revealed by the assessment of prior work in the social sciences. According to C. Herman Pritchett:

Political scientists who have done so much to put the political in "political jurisprudence" need to emphasize that it is still "jurisprudence." It is judging in a political context, but it is still judging; and judging is something different from legislating and administering. . . . Any accurate analysis of judicial behavior must have as a major purpose a full clarification of the unique limiting conditions under which judicial policy making proceeds.[5]

Richard Schwartz made an observation similar to Pritchett's at the conclusion of the conference: "The influences that operate toward uniformity . . . probably constitute a powerful counter weight to variation based on background . . . judicial behavior studies have not—for the most part—asked questions concerning judicial behavior that would be most relevant for the functioning of law in society."[6]

At the same time, the importance of such constraints was being acknowledged by students of symbols and action. The work of major figures in these fields supports the significance of these symbolic constraints. Thus, according to Merleau-Ponty, " . . . our perceptual 'field of presence' is always structured in terms of objects and their relatively but never fully constituted horizons, linked together in a pre-objective order of their own by a constituting consciousness 'which makes explicit and thematizes what was previously presented as only an undetermined horizon.'"[7] Concepts must be so constituted if they are to be claimed under law. In this sense, concepts are not lenses "through which to observe a process that is independent of them," but they constitute political life—they "make it what it is."[8] Since the constraints on perception have been developed with reference to language, the model of language in the judicial decision emphasizes the extent to which that activity is not simply bound by rules, but more fundamentally by conceptual constraints.

It has been shown here that, although some important words are defined in the document and others get elements of their meaning from ordinary use, the context of constitutional interpretation must be examined in order to understand the way words come to have meaning. Because this source of meaning is outside of the traditional investigations of behavioral science, it is offered as a way of filling in symbolic dimensions too often ignored. The investigation began with attention to the ways in which that structure of symbols can be examined. The nature of meaning as consisting of the use of concepts by those for whom it is a form of communication introduced the concept of grammar as a structural constraint on action in a constitutional milieu. In this sense, group life was related to the notion of role as developed in the study of public law, and it was argued that it constituted another element of professional experience akin to the predisposition to follow what has gone before, but operating on the basis of symbols rather than norms. All of this led to the proposition that constitutional law is a linguistic field because it has unique practices which reveal a world distinct from that known by ordinary citizens. These practices affect the decision as a constraint on perception. Some elements of the constraint and potential modes for its investigation are evident in the sense of the constitutional tradition and the criteria by which concepts are known.

Since the special qualities of law that make it of political interest have been minimized throughout much of the discussion, it is worth mentioning some of the ways constitutional symbols operate much as rules, that is, to limit action, without depending on the normative compulsion or the decision to obey.

In law, the possible forms of judicial action and the symbols of the authority of the state are intertwined more deeply than in other spheres. Thus, Scheingold notes, "what we believe about the law is related directly to the legitimacy of our political institutions."[9] The challenge to students of politics in the judicial process is to examine the way in which the symbols operate. By focusing on a sphere, decision-making in the Supreme Court, where the authority of symbols rather than the symbols of authority is the limitation that operates, the investigation of language traverses a domain of considerable significance to political action. Because the legitimacy of the state is based in part on an acceptable body of symbols that indicate the range of institutional action, the sense of these symbols unites the constraints of past policy with those of the policy-making institutions. Since language transforms the needs and feelings of social actors into the "structure of linguistic intersubjectivity," as noted by Habermas,[10] attention to how it operates portrays this transformation. Constitutional law is the language of the structure, and in many cases, it is the substance of American politics. In that sense, the way it operates is not only an example of ideological transformation, but it is itself one of the most significant spheres in which that transformation occurs.

Isaac Balbus has contributed to our understanding of how the structure of meaning is related to the legitimacy of the state. He has characterized the sphere of symbolic legitimacy as one of "legal rationality."[11] It is a characterization that is remarkably similar to that of Edward S. Corwin, who sixty years ago wrote of "the artificial reason" of the law as contributing to the higher law myth that he found as the key to the place of constitutional law in American politics.[12] Such facets of this rationality as due process and equal protection serve to funnel expectations into the established forms through which the state operates. The substance of legal rationality is represented in large part by constitutional law. Although the specific legitimizing role is most evident in the Bill of Rights (and for Balbus in criminal law), the entire structure of government as outlined in the document indicates what sort of action is acceptable. Balbus suggests the way in which this sphere interacts with other values that have to do with the maintenance of order and the perpetuation of institutions. It is important to recognize that the symbolic constraints evident in the constitutional tradition are subject to alteration over time as a result of a variety of political forces.

Deeper investigation into the nature of legal rationality as a tradition of discourse has a bearing in that it addresses the nature of those symbolic constructs without the intervening variable of state authority. The point is that symbols determine the limits of the possible simply because they reveal the accepted ways of proceeding and without the imprimatur of the state. It is important, however, that this body of symbols be maintained by a professional class with the Supreme Court as the final arbiter. Professional standing and the authority of the state reciprocate here in providing a ground for a particular set of symbols that limit the choices and thereby the outcomes open to political actors.

The effort here has not been to explicate the substance of that rationality; this is done adequately by any number of texts on constitutional law. Rather, the point has been that (a) discussions of the Constitution share a common understanding of what is reasonable, even where there is no agreement on what the law is, and that (b) by focusing on how the tradition is used by such important political actors as the Justices of the Supreme Court, we can better understand how that system of rationality itself influences political life.

The introduction of the concept of privacy into the Constitution, for instance, was the culmination of a series of steps by which an ideological value was shaped first in the common law and then in the constitutional setting, so that ultimately the meaning of the concept was such that it might be the basis of a ruling of constitutional standing. Subsequent use had the markings of that process: a close tie to the home, family, and indeed the marital bedroom. By observing the character of such an evolution, students of politics can be better equipped to interpret the conceptual parameters on judicial choice, as well as to anticipate the historical forces that shape the conceptual possibilities in political life. Thus, the model of language use provides a perspective for the study of constitutional law, rich with the conceptual bases of this arena of political life, yet not tied to the parameters themselves. The attention to language also focuses on the spheres in which particular conceptual structures develop. The sphere of constitutional language is only one of the spheres of political life, and as was evident in the arguments in *Brown v. The Board of Education*,[13] the language of another realm, in this case social science, may be introduced to alter a traditional stand of judicial decision.

For those who would alter the constitutional structure, the challenge, then, is the traditional one of law writers and practitioners so inclined. From conservative to progressive, it has been to use the concepts in such a way that they have a new meaning that is still comprehensible. While the prospect for fundamental social change in this area is not good, over time it is not any worse than other avenues of change working with rather than outside the basic social values.

NOTES

1. Connolly, op. cit.; Taylor, op. cit.; Winch, op. cit.
2. Connolly, op. cit., p. 1; see also Martin Shapiro, op. cit., pp. 39–44.

3. Taylor, op. cit.

4. Alfred Schutz, *The Phenomenology of the Social World* (Chicago: Northwestern University Press, 1967), p. 10.

5. C. Herman Pritchett, "The Development of Judicial Research," in Grossman and Tanenhaus, op. cit., p. 42.

6. Richard D. Schwartz, "A Proposed Focus for Research on Judicial Behavior," in Grossman and Tanenhaus, op. cit., p. 490.

7. Maurice Merleau-Ponty, *Signs*, preface by Richard C. McCleary (Chicago: Northwestern University Press, 1964), p. xiii.

8. Connolly, op. cit., p. 180.

9. Scheingold, op. cit., p. 3.

10. Jurgen Habermas, *Legitimation Crisis* (Boston: Beacon Press, 1975), p. 10.

11. Balbus, *The Dialectics of Legal Repression* (New Brunswick, N.J.: Transaction Books, 1977).

12. Edward S. Corwin, *The Higher Law Background of American Constitutional Law* (Reprinted at Ithaca, N.Y.: Cornell University Press, 1967).

13. Op. cit.

Bibliography

BOOKS AND DISSERTATIONS

Allen, Layman E., et al. *Communication Sciences and the Law*. Indianapolis, Ind.: Bobbs-Merrill Co., 1965.

Arnold, Thurman. *The Symbols of Government*. New Haven, Conn.: Yale University Press, 1935.

Austin, J. L. *How to Do Things with Words*. New York: Oxford University Press, 1965.

Ayer, A. J. *Language, Truth and Logic*. New York: Dover, 1946.

Balbus, Isaac. *The Dialectics of Legal Repression*. New Brunswick, N.J.: Transaction Books, 1977.

Bartley, W. W. *Wittgenstein*. Philadelphia: Lippincott, 1973.

Becker, T. L. *Comparative Judicial Politics*. Chicago: Rand McNally and Co., 1970.

――――. *Political Behavioralism and Modern Jurisprudence*. Chicago: Rand McNally, 1964.

Berger, Peter, and Thomas Luckmann. *The Social Construction of Reality*. New York: Doubleday, 1966.

Bishin, William R., and Christopher Stone. *Law, Language and Ethics*. Mineola, N.Y.: Foundation Press, 1972.

Boulding, Kenneth. *The Image*. Ann Arbor, Mich.: University of Michigan Press, 1965.

Brown, Roger. *Monographs of the Society for Research in Child Development*. Vol. 29, No. 1. Chicago: University of Chicago Press, 1964.

Burke, Kenneth. *A Grammar of Motives*. New York: Prentice-Hall, 1945.

Cavell, Stanley. "The Claim to Rationality." Ph.D. Dissertation, Harvard University, 1961–1962.

――――. *Must We Mean What We Say?* New York: Charles Scribner's, 1969.

Chase, Stuart. *The Tyranny of Words*. New York: Harcourt, Brace and Co., 1939.

Chomsky, Noam. *Aspects of a Theory of Syntax.* Cambridge, Mass.: M.I.T. Press, 1965.

―――. *Current Issues in Linguistic Theory.* The Hague: Monton and Co., 1964.

―――. *Language and Mind.* New York: Harcourt, Brace and Co., 1968.

Connolly, William E. *The Terms of Political Discourse.* Lexington, Mass.: D. C. Heath, 1974.

Cooley, Thomas M. *Treatise on Torts.* 2nd ed. Chicago: Callaghan and Co., 1888.

Corwin, Edward S. *The Higher Law Background of American Constitutional Law.* rpt. Ithaca, N.Y.: Cornell University Press, 1967.

Crosskey, W. W. *Politics and the Constitution in the History of the United States.* Chicago: University of Chicago Press, 1953.

Dixon, Robert G. *The Right of Privacy.* New York: DaCapo Press, 1971.

Dworkin, Ronald. *Taking Rights Seriously.* Cambridge, Mass.: Harvard University Press, 1976.

Edelman, Murray. *Political Language.* New York: Academic Press, 1977.

―――. *Politics as Symbolic Action: Mass Arousal and Quiescence.* New York: Academic Press, 1971.

―――. *The Symbolic Uses of Politics.* Urbana, Ill.: University of Illinois Press, 1964.

Eulau, Heinz. *The Behavioral Persuasion in Politics.* New York: Random House, 1963.

Flathman, Richard E. *Political Obligation.* New York: Atheneum, 1972.

―――. *The Practice of Rights.* Cambridge: Cambridge University Press, 1977.

Fodor, Jerry A., and Jerrold J. Katz. *The Structure of Language.* Englewood Cliffs, N.J.: Prentice-Hall, 1964.

Frank, Jerome. *Law and the Modern Mind.* New York: Brentano's, 1930.

Fuller, Lon. *Legal Fictions.* Stanford, Calif.: Stanford University Press, 1967.

Garfinkel, Harold. *Studies in Ethnomethodology.* Englewood Cliffs, N.J.: Prentice-Hall, 1967.

Garvey, Gerald. *Constitutional Bricolage.* Princeton, N.J.: Princeton University Press, 1971.

Goldman, Sheldon. *The Federal Courts as a Political System.* 2nd edition. New York: Harper and Row, 1976.

Gottlieb, Gidon. *The Logic of Choice.* London: Allen and Unwin, 1968.

Gunnell, John. *Philosophy, Science and Political Inquiry.* Morristown, N.J.: General Learning Press, 1975.

Gunther, Gerald. *Cases on Constitutional Law.* Mineola, N.Y.: Foundation Press, 1976.

Habermas, Jurgen. *Legitimation Crisis.* Boston: Beacon Press, 1975.

Hall, Jerome. *Living Law of Democratic Society.* Indianapolis, Ind.: Bobbs-Merrill Co., 1949.

Harrison, Bernard. *Form and Content.* Oxford: Basil Blackwell, 1973.

———. *Meaning and Structure: An Essay in the Philosophy of Language.* New York: Harper and Row, 1972.

Hart, H.L.A. *The Concept of Law.* New York: Oxford University Press, 1960.

Hohfeld, Wesley N. *Fundamental Legal Conceptions.* New Haven, Conn.: Yale University Press, 1919.

Holmes, Oliver Wendell. *Collected Legal Papers.* New York: Harcourt, Brace and Howe, 1920.

Janik, Allen, and Stephen Toulmin. *Wittgenstein's Vienna.* New York: Simon and Schuster, 1973.

Karlen, Delmar. *The Citizen in Court.* New York: Holt, Rinehart and Winston, 1964.

Katz, Jerrold J. *The Philosophy of Language.* New York: Harper and Row, 1966.

Kelsen, Hans. *Pure Theory of Law.* Berkeley: University of California Press, 1967.

Krislov, Samuel. *The Supreme Court in the Political Process.* New York: Macmillan Co., 1965.

Kuhn, Thomas. *The Structure of Scientific Revolutions.* Chicago: University of Chicago Press, 1962.

Lakoff, Robin. *Language and Woman's Place.* New York: Harper and Row, 1975.

Lasswell, Harold. *Politics, Who Gets What, When, How?* New York: Meridan, 1958.

Levi, Edward. *An Introduction to Legal Reasoning.* Chicago: University of Chicago Press, 1948.

Lewis, Anthony. *Gideon's Trumpet.* New York: Vintage Books, 1964.

Lyas, Colin. *Philosophy and Linguistics.* London: Macmillan, 1971.

Marcuse, Herbert. *One Dimensional Man.* Boston: Beacon Press, 1964.

Mellinkoff, David. *The Language of the Law.* Boston: Little, Brown and Co., 1963.

Mencken, H. L. *The American Language.* New York: Knopf, 1977.

Merleau-Ponty, Maurice. *Signs.* Chicago: Northwestern University Press, 1964.

Mowrer, O. Hobart. *Learning Theory and the Symbolic Processes.* New York: John Wiley, 1960.

Mueller, Claus. *The Politics of Communication.* London: Oxford University Press, 1973.

Murphy, Walter, and C. Herman Pritchett. *Courts, Judges and Politics: An Introduction to the Judicial Process*. New York: Random House, 1961.

Osgood, C. E. *Method and Theory in Experimental Psychology*. New York: Oxford University Press, 1953.

Passmore, John. *A Hundred Years of Philosophy*. Baltimore: Penguin Books, 1957.

Pears, David. *Ludwig Wittgenstein*. New York: Viking Press, 1969.

Perelman, Chaim. *The Idea of Justice and the Problem of Argument*. New York: Humanities Press, 1963.

Philbrick, Frederick A. *Language and the Law*. New York: Macmillan Co., 1949.

Pitkin, Hannah. *Wittgenstein and Justice*. Berkeley: University of California Press, 1972.

Piven, Frances F., and Richard A. Cloward. *Regulating the Poor*. New York: Pantheon, 1971.

Pranger, Robert. *Action, Symbolism and Order*. Nashville, Tenn.: Vanderbilt University Press, 1968.

Pritchett, Herman C. *The American Constitution*. New York: McGraw-Hill, 1959.

———. *Civil Liberties and the Vinson Court*. Chicago: University of Chicago Press, 1954.

———. *The Political Offender and the Warren Court*. Boston: Boston University Press, 1958.

———. *The Roosevelt Court: A Study in Judicial Politics and Values, 1937–1947*. New York: Macmillan Co., 1948.

Probert, Walter. *Law, Language and Communication*. Springfield, Ill.: Charles C. Thomas, 1972.

Quine, W.V.O. *Word and Object*. Cambridge, Mass.: M.I.T. Press, 1960.

Renner, Karl. *The Institutions of Private Law and Their Social Function*. Ed. O. Kahn-Freund. London: Routledge and Kegan Paul, 1949.

Rich, Francis M., Jr. "Role Perception and Precedent Orientation as Variables Influencing Appellate Judicial Decision Making: An Analysis of the Fifth Circuit Court of Appeals." Ph.D. Dissertation, University of Georgia, 1967.

Rohde, David. W., and Harold J. Spaeth. *Supreme Court Decision Making*. San Francisco: W. H. Freeman and Co., 1976.

Ross, Alf. *On Law and Justice*. London: Stevens and Sons, Ltd., 1958.

Ryle, Gilbert. *The Concept of Mind*. New York: Barnes and Noble, 1949.

Saint Augustine. *Confessions*. I. 8.

Schaff, Adam. *Language and Cognition*. New York: McGraw-Hill, 1973.

Scheingold, Stuart. *The Politics of Rights.* New Haven, Conn.: Yale University Press, 1974.

Schubert, Glendon. *Human Jurisprudence: Public Law as Political Science.* Honolulu: University Press of Hawaii, 1975.

———. *The Judicial Mind.* Evanston, Ill.: Northwestern University Press, 1965.

———. *The Judicial Mind Revisited.* New York: Oxford University Press, 1974.

———. *Quantitative Analysis of Judicial Behavior.* New York: Free Press, 1959.

Schutz, Alfred. *The Phenomenology of the Social World.* Chicago: Northwestern University Press, 1967.

Schwyzer, Hubert. "The Acquisition of Concepts and the Use of Language." Ph.D. Dissertation, University of California, Berkeley, 1968.

Shapiro, Martin. *The Supreme Court and Administrative Agencies.* New York: Free Press, 1968.

Shklar, Judith. *Legalism.* Cambridge, Mass.: Harvard University Press, 1964.

Simon, Herbert. *Administrative Behavior.* 2nd edition. New York: Macmillan, 1957.

Skinner, B. F. *Verbal Behavior.* New York: Appleton-Century-Crofts, 1957.

Spaeth, Harold. *An Introduction to Supreme Court Decision Making.* Revised edition. San Francisco: Chandler, 1972.

Stone, Julius. *Law and the Social Sciences in the Second Half Century.* Minneapolis: University of Minnesota, 1966.

———. *Legal System and Lawyer's Reasonings.* Stanford, Calif.: Stanford University Press, 1964.

Toulmin, Stephen. *The Uses of Argument.* Cambridge: Cambridge University Press, 1964.

Unger, Roberto. *Law in Modern Society.* New York: Free Press, 1976.

Wahlke, John L., et al. *The Legislative System.* New York: John Wiley, 1962.

Waismann, Frederick. *Principles of Linguistic Philosophy.* London: Macmillan, 1965.

Wasby, Stephen. *Continuity and Change.* Pacific Palisades, Calif.: Goodyear Publishing Co., 1976.

Wasserstrom, Richard. *The Judicial Decision.* Stanford: Stanford University Press, 1961.

Winch, Peter. *The Idea of a Social Science.* London: Routledge and Kegan Paul, 1958.

Wisdom, John. *Philosophy and Psycho-analysis.* Berkeley: University of California Press, 1969.

Wittgenstein, Ludwig. *Blue and Brown Books.* New York: Harper and Row, 1964.

————. *On Certainty.* New York: Harper and Row, 1969.

————. *Philosophical Investigations.* New York: Macmillan Co., 1958.

————. *Tractatus Logico-Philosophicus.* London: Routledge and Kegan Paul, 1961.

ARTICLES

Albritton, Rogers. "On Wittgenstein's Use of the Term 'Criterion'." In *Wittgenstein, The Philosophical Investigations.* Ed. George Pitcher. New York: Anchor Books, 1966.

Beaney, William M. "The Constitutional Right to Privacy." *Supreme Court Review* (1962):212-251.

Becker, Theodore L. "A Survey Study of Hawaiian Judges: The Effect on Decisions of Judicial Role Variations." *American Political Science Review* 60 (September 1966): 677-681.

Beutel, Frederick K. "Elementary Semantics: Critique of Realism and Experimental Jurisprudence." *Journal of Legal Education* 13 (1960): 67-76. "The Relationship of Experimental Jurisprudence to Other Schools of Jurisprudence and the Scientific Method." *Washington University Law Quarterly* 71 (1971): 385.

Blawie, James L., and Marilyn J. Blawie. "The Judicial Decision: A Second Look at Certain Assumptions of Behavioral Research." *Western Political Quarterly* 18 (1965): 579-593.

Bodenheimer, Edgar. "A Neglected Theory of Legal Reasoning." *Journal of Legal Education* 21 (1969): 373-402.

Canfield, John V. "Criteria and Rules of Language." *Philosophical Review* 1 (1974): 70-87.

Chafee, Zechariah. "The Disorderly Conduct of Words." *Columbia Law Review* 41 (1941): 381-404.

Chomsky, Noam. "Review of *Verbal Behavior.*" *Language* 35 (1959): 26-58.

Cohen, Saul. "Justice Holmes and Copyright Law." *ETC.* 23 (December 1966): 439-461.

Cohen, Felix. "Transcendental Nonsense and the Functional Approach." *Columbia Law Review* 35 (1935): 809-849.

Cowan, Thomas A. "Decision Theory in Law, Science and Technology." *Rutgers Law Review* 17 (1963): 499.

Dahl, Robert. "The Behavioral Approach in Political Science: Epitaph for a Monument to a Successful Protest." In *Behavioralism in Political Science.* Ed. Heinz Eulau. New York: Atherton Press, 1969.

Danet, Brenda. "The Role of Language in the Legal Process." N.S.F. Grant (1975).

Dworkin, Ronald, "The Model of Rules." *University of Chicago Law Review* 35 (1967): 14–46.

———. "Social Rules and Legal Theory." *Yale Law Journal* 81 (1972):3.

Easton, David. "The New Revolution in Political Science." *American Political Science Review* 63 (1969): 1051–1061.

Editorial. *New York Times*, March 31, 1976.

Emerson, Thomas I. "Nine Justices in Search of a Doctrine." In *The Right of Privacy.* New York: DaCapo Press, 1971.

Epstein, Richard A. "Substantive Due Process by Any Other Name: The Abortion Cases." *Supreme Court Review* (1973).

Fahlund, G. Gregory. "Retroactivity and the Warren Court." *Journal of Politics* 34 (1973):570–593.

Flango, Victor E., and Craig R. Ducat. "Toward an Integration of Public Law and Judicial Behavior." *Journal of Politics* 39 (1977): 41–72.

Gifford, Daniel J. "Communication of Legal Standards." *Cornell Law Review* 56 (1971): 426–430.

———. "Decisions, Decisional Referents and Administrative Justice." *Law and Contemporary Problems* 37 (Winter 1972): 3.

Goldman, Sheldon. "Conflict on the U.S. Courts of Appeals 1965–1971: A Quantitative Analysis." *University of Cincinnati Law Review* 42 (1973): 635–658.

Griswold, Erwin N. "The Right to Be Let Alone." *Northwestern University Law Review* 55 (1960): 216.

Grossman, Joel B. "Social Backgrounds and Judicial Decisions: Notes for a Theory." *Journal of Politics* 29 (1967): 334–351.

Hart, H.L.A. "Definition and Theory in Jurisprudence." *Law Quarterly Review* 70 (1954): 37–60.

Hohfeld, Wesley N. "Some Fundamental Legal Conceptions as Applied in Judicial Reasoning." *Yale Law Journal* 23 (1913): 16–59.

Hunter, J.F.M. "Wittgenstein on Meaning and Use." In *Essays on Wittgenstein.* Ed. E. D. Klemke. Urbana Ill.: University of Illinois Press, 1971: 273–297.

Lewis, Ovid C., et al. "Symposium: Law, Language and Communication." *Case Western Reserve Law Review* 23 (Winter 1972):307–317.

Malcolm, N. "Anselm's Ontological Argument." *Philosophical Review* 69 (1960): 389-394.

Northrup, F.S.C. "Law, Language and Morals." *Yale Law Journal* 71 (May 1962): 1017-1048.

Oldenquist, Andrew. "Wittgenstein on Phenomenalism, Skepticism, and Criteria." In *Essays on Wittgenstein*. Ed. E. D. Klemke. Urbana, Ill.: University of Illinois Press, 1971.

Pritchett, C. Herman. "The Development of Judicial Research." In *The Frontiers of Judicial Research*. Eds. Joel Grossman and Joseph Tanenhaus. New York: John Wiley and Sons, 1969.

———. "Divisions of Opinion Among Justices of the United States Supreme Court, 1939-41." *American Political Science Review* 35 (1941): 890-898.

Probert, Walter. "Law and Persuasion: The Language Behavior of Lawyers." *University of Pennsylvania Law Review* (1959): 35-58.

———. "Law Through the Looking Glass of Language and Communication Behavior." *Journal of Legal Education* 20 (1968): 253.

———. "Symposium on Law, Language and Communication." *Western Reserve Law Review* 9 (1958): 115.

Rawls, John. "Two Concepts of Rules." *Philosophical Review* 64 (1955): 3-32.

Rokeach, Milton. "The Nature of Attitudes." *International Encyclopedia of the Social Sciences*, Vol. 1, 1968., pp. 449-457.

Ryle, Gilbert. "Use, Usage and Meaning." *Proceedings of the Aristotelian Society,* Suppl. Vol. 35 (1961): 223-230.

Sartorius, Rolf. "The Justification of the Judicial Decision." *Ethics* 78, (1968): 171.

Schlick, Moritz. "Meaning and Verification." *Philosophical Review* 45 (1936): 339-369.

Schubert, Glendon. "Civilian Control and Stare Decisis in the Warren Court." In *Judicial Decision-Making*. Ed. Glendon Schubert. New York: Free Press, 1963.

———. "Judicial Attitudes and Voting Behavior." *Law and Contemporary Problems* 28 (Winter 1963): 100-142.

———. "Prediction from a Psychometric Model." In *Judicial Behavior*. Ed. Glendon Schubert. Chicago: Rand McNally and Co., 1964.

———. "A Psychological Model of Supreme Court Decision-Making." In *Judicial Behavior*. Ed. Glendon Schubert. Chicago: Rand McNally and Co., 1964.

———. "The Rhetoric of Constitutional Change." *Journal of Public Law* 16 (1967): 16-50.

————. "The Study of Judicial Decision-Making as an Aspect of Political Behavior." *American Political Science Review* 52 (1958): 1007–1025.

Schwartz, Richard D. "A Proposed Focus for Research on Judicial Behavior." In *The Frontiers of Judicial Research*. Eds. Joel Grossman and Joseph Tanenhaus. New York: John Wiley and Sons, 1969.

Schwyzer, Hubert. "Rules and Practices." *Philosophical Review* (October 1969): 451–467.

Searle, John. "How to Derive 'Ought' from 'Is'." In *Theories of Ethics*. Ed. Phillipa Foot. New York: Oxford University Press, 1967.

Shapiro, Martin. "Political Jurisprudence." *Kentucky Law Journal* 55 (1963–64): 294–343.

————. "Toward a Theory of Stare Decisis." *Journal of Legal Studies* 1 (January 1972): 125–134.

Smith, J. C. "Law, Language and Philosophy." *University of British Columbia Law Review* (May 1968): 59.

Stroud, B. "Wittgenstein and Logical Necessity." In *Essays on Wittgenstein*. Ed. E. D. Klemke. Urbana, Ill.: University of Illinois Press, 1971.

Tanenhaus, Joseph, et al. "The Supreme Court's Certiorari Jurisdiction: Cue Theory." In *Judidicial Decision-Making*. Ed. Glendon Schubert. New York: Free Press, 1963.

Taylor, Charles. "Interpretation and the Sciences of Man." *Review of Metaphysics* 25 (September 1971): 3–51.

Toulmin, Stephen. "Wittgenstein." *Encounter* 32 (1969): 58–71.

Ulmer, S. S. "The Discriminant Function and a Theoretical Context for Its Use in Estimating the Votes of Judges." In *The Frontiers of Judicial Research*. Eds. Joel Grossman and Joseph Tanenhaus. New York: John Wiley and Sons, 1969.

————. "Dissent Behavior and the Social Background of Supreme Court Justices." *Journal of Politics* 32 (1970): 580–599.

Vines, Kenneth. "The Judicial Role in American States." In *The Frontiers of Judicial Research*. Eds. Joel Grossman and Joseph Tanenhaus. New York: John Wiley and Sons, 1969.

Waismann, F. "Verifiability." Reprinted in *Logic and Language*. Ed. Anthony Flew. New York: Doubleday and Co., 1965.

Warren, Samuel D., and Louis Brandeis. "The Right to Privacy." *Harvard Law Review* 4 (1890): 193.

Williams, G. "Language and the Law." *Law Quarterly Review* 61 (1945): 71–86, 179–95, 293–303, 284–406.

Wittgenstein, Ludwig. "Notes for Lectures on 'Private Experience' and Sense Data." *Philosophical Review* 77 (1968): 275–320.

Zabeeh, Farhang. "On Language Games and Forms of Life." In *Essays on Wittgenstein.* Ed. E. D. Klemke. Urbana, Ill.: University of Illinois Press, 1971.

Zeisel, Hans. " . . . And Then There Were None: The Diminution of the Federal Jury." *University of Chicago Law Review* 38 (1971): 710.

COURT CASES

Adamson v. California. 322 U.S. 46. 1947.

Apodaca v. Oregon. 406 U.S. 404. 1972.

Argersinger v. Hamlin. 407 U.S. 25. 1972.

Betts v. Brady. 316 U.S. 455. 1942.

Boyd v. U.S. 116 U.S. 616. 1886.

Bram v. U.S. 168 U.S. 532. 1897.

Brown v. Board of Education. 347 U.S. 483. 1954.

Buckley v. Valeo. 96 S. Ct. 612. 1976.

Caminetti v. U.S. 242 U.S. 470. 1917.

Covington Bridge Co. v. Kentucky. 154 U.S. 204. 1894.

Cox Broadcasting Corporation v. Cohn. 420 U.S. 469. 1975.

Doe v. Commonwealth's Attorney for the City of Richmond. 96 S. Ct. 1489. 1976.

Dupont v. John F. Finklea. U.S. District Court for the Southern District of West Virginia. December 20, 1977.

Eisenstadt v. Baird. 405 U.S. 438. 1972.

Furman v. Georgia. 408 U.S. 238. 1976.

Garner v. Louisiana. 368 U.S. 157. 1961.

Gibbons v. Ogden. 9 Wheat. 1. 1824.

Gideon v. Wainwright. 372 U.S. 335. 1963.

Goldman v. U.S. 316 U.S. 129. 1942.

Gregg v. Georgia. 428 U.S. 153. 1972.

Griswold v. Connecticut. 381 U.S. 479. 1965.

Katz v. U.S. 389 U.S. 347. 1967.

Katzenbach v. McClung. 379 U.S. 294. 1964.

Kelley v. Johnson. 96 S. Ct. 1440. 1976.

Lochner v. New York. 198 U.S. 45. 1905.

Miranda v. Arizona. 384 U.S. 436. 1966.

Mitchell v. U.S. 313 U.S. 80. 1941.

Moose Lodge No. 107 v Irvis. 407 U.S. 163. 1972.

Olmstead v. U.S. 277 U.S. 438. 1928.

Palko v. Connecticut. 302 U.S. 319. 1937.

Paris Adult Theatre I v. Slaton. 413 U.S. 49. 1973.

Paul v. Davis. 96 S. Ct. 1155. 1976.

Planned Parenthood v. Danforth. 96 S. Ct. 2831. 1976.

Plessy v. Ferguson. 163 U.S. 537. 1896.

Pollak v. Public Utilities Commission. 191 F. 2nd. 450. 1951.

PUC v. Pollak. 343 U.S. 451. 1951.

Rochin v. California. 342 U.S. 165. 1952.

Roe v. Wade. 410 U.S. 113. 1973.

Silverman v. U.S. 365 U.S. 505. 1961.

Stanley v. Georgia. 394 U.S. 557. 1969.

Stein v. New York. 346 U.S. 156. 1953.

Time, Inc. v. Firestone. 96 S. Ct. 958. 1970.

Towne v. Eisner. 245 U.S. 418, 425. 1918.

U.S. v. Bass. 404 U.S. 336. 1971.

U.S. v. Darby Lumber Co. 312 U.S. 100. 1941.

U.S. v. Reidel. 402 U.S. 351. 1971.

Village of Belle Terre v. Boraos. 416 U.S. 1. 1974.

Weems v. U.S. 217 U.S. 349. 1910.

Whalen v. Roe. 429 U.S. 589. 1977.

Williams v. Florida. 399 U.S. 78. 1970.

Wolf v. Colorado. 338 U.S. 25. 1949.

Index